Springer Series in Healthcare Management and Innovation

The Springer Series in Healthcare Management and Innovation presents a curated collection of research monographs, contributed volumes, and professional titles that illuminate emerging theories, empirical studies, practical applications, strategic frameworks, and real-world case studies in healthcare. Each volume addresses a broad spectrum of topics in healthcare management and innovation, including—but not limited to—leadership, financial management, ethics and corporate social responsibility (CSR), human resource management, managed care, workforce and patient diversity, research and development (R&D) of medical technologies, organizational strategy and planning, and healthcare information systems.

By bridging the gap between theory and practice, this series serves as an essential resource for academics, researchers, scholars, and practitioners. It equips readers with the insights and competencies needed to navigate and lead effectively in the dynamic and evolving landscape of healthcare.

Bandar Alknawy
Editor

Organizational Insights: Healthcare Perspective

An Introduction to the Dynamics of Healthcare Excellence

Springer

Editor
Bandar Alknawy
Ministry of National Guard Health Affairs (MNGHA)
Riyadh, Saudi Arabia

ISSN 3091-3810 ISSN 3091-3829 (electronic)
Springer Series in Healthcare Management and Innovation
ISBN 978-3-032-10531-8 ISBN 978-3-032-10532-5 (eBook)
https://doi.org/10.1007/978-3-032-10532-5

This work was supported by Ministry of National Guard Health Affairs.

This Springer imprint is published by the registered company Springer Nature Switzerland AG
The registered company address is: Gewerbestrasse 11, 6330 Cham, Switzerland

Foreword

In the ever-evolving healthcare landscape, the pursuit of excellence demands more than reactive strategies, which require a forward-thinking mindset rooted in the principle of "Insights for Foresight," the running theme of this exciting healthcare news. This strategic concept is a guiding philosophy and a transformative approach that empowers organizations to navigate uncertainty, forecast future difficulties, and seize opportunities for continuing success. Healthcare leaders can light the path by adopting this idea and creating a vision for innovation, resilience, and growth. Indeed, this philosophy encompasses the tenets of proactivity by empowering organizations to leapfrog traditional barriers, anticipate emerging trends, and articulate their vision toward a future of continuous advancement and excellence.

To illustrate this mission, I draw inspiration from "Point Nemo," the most remote location on Earth, known as the modern "oceanic pole of inaccessibility." Much like this obscure point, the pinnacle of organizational achievement in healthcare lies far beyond the horizon of conventional thinking. It is a destination that demands bold vision, unwavering commitment, and the ability to transform present insights into future foresight.

The essence of Insights for Foresight lies in the continuous generation, refinement, and elevation of knowledge. Insights are not static; they are dynamic, shaped by diverse perspectives, experiences, and the intricacies of human cognition. They spring from data-driven analysis and instinctive understanding, empathy, and the ability to perceive beyond the obvious.

The journey to Point Nemo is not a solitary endeavor but a collective marathon toward excellence. It requires leaders and their teams to forge ahead together, united by a shared vision and a commitment to continuous improvement. This expedition is a drive to explore new frontiers, redefine possibilities, and lead with purpose.

Ultimately, Insights for Foresight is more than just a management practice. It is a call to action for healthcare leaders to pioneer new pathways, inspire their teams, and redefine possibilities. Let this vision guide us as we navigate the complexities of healthcare, transforming insights into foresight and foresight into a legacy of distinction. Together, we can reach the farthest edges of achievement, where the future is not just imagined but actively shaped by the insights of today.

Ministry of National Guard Health Affairs
Riyadh, Saudi Arabia

Bandar Alknawy

Preface

Organizational Insights: Healthcare Perspective is a comprehensive exploration into the intricate frameworks that shape modern healthcare. This book delves into the challenges and opportunities within healthcare organizations, addressing the interplay between management practices, technological advancements, work culture, and policy-making. With a focus on enhancing healthcare outcomes, it draws from the personal expertise of the authors, extensive research, and real-world insights, aiming to provide readers with actionable strategies to improve both the quality and efficiency of healthcare services. To this end, the book is not an academic summary of current research, but serves as a practical guide, offering insights into how effective organizational structures can make a substantial difference in patient care and operational success.

The first section, "Organizational Insights," examines the foundational principles of healthcare management and structure. This section offers a rich understanding of what makes some healthcare organizations thrive, with key insights that illustrate the points made.

As one of the key modern tools in the organizational transformation in healthcare, digitalization is the main aspect of the section "Digitalization Insights," which explores the transformative impact of digital technology on healthcare delivery and administration. This section highlights how digital tools—from electronic health records to artificial intelligence—are reshaping the way healthcare organizations operate.

The third section delves into various models of organizational insight of the people involved in delivering healthcare, in particular the behaviors and leadership that directly impact patient outcomes, workforce satisfaction, and operational efficiencies. By analyzing successful case studies, topics such as decision-making and stakeholder engagement are discussed in depth, showing how these elements interconnect within healthcare settings.

The fourth section, "Technology and Policy Alignment," addresses the critical need for coherent strategies that integrate technological innovation with existing policies. In the current era where technology is advancing at an unprecedented rate, healthcare organizations face the dual challenge of adopting new technologies while navigating regulatory requirements. This section explores how aligning technology with policy can streamline processes, improve patient outcomes, and reduce costs.

Finally, the book concludes with the "Future perspectives" including practical guidance on implementation and examining how the insights offered can enhance healthcare delivery. The book illustrates the tangible benefits of digital transformation, providing examples of hospitals and clinics that have leveraged digitalization to improve patient outcomes and streamline operations.

The background experiences of the lead authors have been critical in shaping this book, as they represent different viewpoints, from the executive views of running complex healthcare organizations, to frontline clinicians, to healthcare infrastructure and pharmaceutical company leaders. Yet, they all coalesce toward the insights offered, providing a unique opportunity to interrogate and integrate those viewpoints. Taken together, these insights position readers to better navigate the rapidly evolving landscape of digital healthcare. By reviewing the successful examples given, for example in digitization and technology-policy alignment, this book offers a blueprint for healthcare leaders to ensure that technological upgrades comply with, and even enhance, policy frameworks.

Riyadh, Saudi Arabia Bandar Alknawy

Contents

1 **Organizational Insights: Uncovering the Essence and Principles** 1
Bandar Alknawy
1.1 Overview of Organizational Insights 1
1.2 Communicating Organizational Insights 2
1.3 Principles of Organizational Insights 3
1.4 Insight Effects 4
1.5 Insight Content 6
1.6 The Delphi Method and Insights 6
1.7 Conspicuous Insights 8
1.8 Five Powerful Methods for Growth and Innovation 9
References 10

2 **Digital Insights** 13
Karine Sargsyan
2.1 Leveraging Technology in Healthcare 16
2.2 Addressing Challenges in Digital Healthcare Transformation 17
2.2.1 Key Challenges in Digital Healthcare Transformation 17
2.2.2 Technological Barriers 18
2.2.3 Regulatory and Compliance Issues 19
2.2.4 Cultural Resistance 20
2.2.5 Data Security and Privacy Concerns 21
2.3 Strategies for Successful Transformation 21
2.3.1 Change Management Approaches 22
2.3.2 Lessons Learned from Failure 22
2.3.3 Ethical Issues 23
2.3.4 Informed Consent in Digital Interventions 23
2.4 Enhancing Organizational Efficiency 24
2.5 Innovations in Digital Healthcare Solutions 28
References 31

3 **Organization of People and Behavioral Insights** 35
Angeliki Koltsida, Io Hong Cheong, and Zisis Kozlakidis
3.1 Leadership Styles and Healthcare 36
3.2 Team Dynamics and Interdisciplinary Collaboration 38

3.3 Talent Acquisition and Recruitment Strategies 40
3.4 Employee Training and Development Programs: Engagement and Motivation 40
3.5 Performance Management and Appraisal Systems 42
3.6 Where Do Things Go Wrong? 43
3.7 Challenges and Insights on How to Fix Them 45
References 46

4 Insights for Resilient and Patient-Centric Healthcare Systems 49
Liz Sparacino and Annette Schmid
4.1 The Importance of Resilient Health Systems 49
4.1.1 Patient Access to Healthcare 50
4.1.2 The Need for Policy 51
4.2 System Flexibility with Technology 51
4.2.1 Risks to Be Considered in the Context of Technology Use in Healthcare 54
4.2.2 Policy Alignment and Coordination 55
4.3 Patient Centricity and Careful Evaluation of Community Needs . . . 57
4.3.1 Evaluation Through an Ethics of Care Approach 57
4.3.2 Exploring Ethics of Care in Practice 58
4.3.3 The Patient Experience with Healthcare Technology 58
4.3.4 Prospective and Sustained Community Engagement 59
4.4 Emerging Insights on Resilient Healthcare Centers and Their Providers 60
4.5 Ensuring Future Successful Technology and Policy Alignment in Healthcare Systems 62
4.5.1 Affordability and Practicality of Technology 62
4.5.2 Our Recommendations 63
References 65

5 Future Perspective Insights: Healthcare and Medical Sciences 69
Karine Sargsyan
5.1 Introduction 69
5.1.1 Background and Rationale for the Future of Healthcare Organization 70
5.2 Understanding Organizational Peculiarities of Future Planning in Healthcare 71
5.2.1 Structural Characteristics 72
5.3 Challenges and Opportunities in Healthcare Organizations in the Near Future 73
5.3.1 Technological Advancements 73
5.4 Impact of Organizational Specifics on Patient Care 74
5.5 Future Directions and Innovations 75
5.5.1 Artificial Intelligence in Healthcare 75
5.5.2 Other Technological Advances 75

5.6 Conclusion and Recommendations 79
5.6.1 Global Recommendations and Detailed Implementation Roadmap for Healthcare Digitalization 79
References 87

Organizational Insights: Uncovering the Essence and Principles

1

Bandar Alknawy

Organizational Insights (OIs) is a term that can be used to define and differentiate one organization from another. Its purpose is to outline an organization's distinct identity, within which a unique imprint can be pinpointed both internally and externally. More specifically, OIs have the ability to shape holistic themes and create a platform for strategic innovation, competitive performance, and optimized processes to achieve success. These types of insights are crucial, as they serve as foundational knowledge that enables an organization to capitalize on its unique capabilities, traditions, and exceptional assets and values. Insights are an integral component for organizational improvement and can enhance an organization's sustainability, success, and innovative growth. Some of their critical roles include interpreting and perceiving information to create transformative environments for organizations.

1.1 Overview of Organizational Insights

A simple way of looking at OIs is by comparing them to DNA, which, as we all know, defines and shapes organisms. Through questioning and introspection, OIs aim to determine an organization's strengths, weaknesses, and underlying principles guiding its actions. To pursue such an endeavor requires the ability to recognize and aspire to ideal forms that encompass efficiency, collaboration, and purpose. Once this level of understanding has been achieved, a creative platform can be realized to

B. Alknawy (✉)
Ministry of National Guard Health Affairs (MNGHA), Riyadh, Kingdom of Saudi Arabia

King Abdullah International Medical Research Center (KAIMRC), Riyadh, Saudi Arabia

King Saud Bin Abdulaziz University for Health Sciences (KSAU-HS), Riyadh, Saudi Arabia
e-mail: knawyb@mngha.med.sa

B. Alknawy (ed.), *Organizational Insights: Healthcare Perspective*, Springer Series in Healthcare Management and Innovation,
https://doi.org/10.1007/978-3-032-10532-5_1

facilitate strategic innovation, competitive performance, and optimized processes, all of which help achieve long-term organizational excellence.

The fundamental and enduring aspects of an organization is to create a foundation for stability and sustainability. This is where data-driven OIs come to light, as they unveil the crucial but often hidden patterns that are paramount for effective long-term strategy. Having said that, we cannot solely rely on data. Instead, we must take into account an institution's collective wisdom and experience, which can be achieved by analyzing a company's employees. For instance, having a nuanced understanding of collaboration, communication, and shared knowledge among team members is absolutely necessary when considering optimal workflows. This non-data image of OIs encompasses a tacit understanding of workflows, the ability to navigate various complexities, and a level of intuition that comes from an amalgamation of experience and expertise.

When these attributes are combined, it creates a solid foundation to propel informed decision-making and innovation and also helps build a resilient organizational culture. In essence, the non-data side to OIs is what combines the necessary elements for an organization to succeed. With this in mind, it is vital for an organization to have a clear understanding of economic dynamics and their impact on an organization. However, since these dynamics interplay with social and leadership factors, we must take a holistic approach to understanding and managing organizations.

1.2 Communicating Organizational Insights

Public perception can be influenced by a number of factors, such as communication strategies, transparency, and consistency. Furthermore, publicizing insights can contribute to an organization's reputation and relationships with stakeholders. By choosing to openly share valuable information, organizations can position themselves as leaders, foster trust, and contribute positively to their communities. In terms of shaping and understanding public perception, the dynamic between insights and authenticity in an organizational context is a reciprocal relationship. Authenticity fosters an environment that is conducive to generating meaningful insights. These insights then contribute to an authentic organizational culture, thereby creating a foundation for free-flowing communication, trust, and diversity of thought. All these components are essential for generating valuable insights that enhance public perception. Insights contribute to an authentic culture by providing tangible evidence of an organization's commitment to learning, improving, and being diverse. Similarly, the reciprocal relationship between insights and intuitive decision-making contributes to a clear understanding of organizational challenges and opportunities. When effectively integrated, they can enhance decision-making processes and contribute to organizational success.

1.3 Principles of Organizational Insights

Organizational insights are achieved by considering a number of processes. The principles of observation, experimentation, and critical thinking have the potential to be inspirational for organizations seeking effective and informed management practices. Adopting evidence-based decision-making provides an opportunity to foster a culture of inquiry and prioritize systematic approaches to problem-solving. These principles, can be a foundation of inspiration for organizations seeking effective and informed management practices. Ethical considerations must also be included, especially to encourage staff within organizations to prioritize values and integrity in their operations. Within this line of thought, emphasizing clear communication and interconnectedness is crucial, as it encourages collaboration and coordination within an organization.

Having trust in OIs is a multifaceted concept that involves not only the accuracy of data but also transparency, consistency, ethical considerations, and the ability to incorporate user feedback. Among such considerations, we must appreciate and embrace diversity and change while also projecting a global mindset. Having a better understanding of different cultures and environments allows us to put forward more flexible and resilient organizational strategies. Being committed to further education about diversity is a solid example of how an organization can align its values with the team.

OIs are dynamic and continuously evolving, and they have undoubtedly been influenced by different time periods and generations. For instance, each generation leaves a unique imprint on OIs through historical, cultural, and social norms and values, as well as priorities and intellectual progress. Generational alternation and succession may have a detrimental impact and might even be a catalyst that drives performance, resilience, and competitiveness. This profound effect offers a unique perspective on professionalism and managerial practices.

There is indeed a generational influence on the future of OIs, along with the expectations surrounding the ability to maintain an organization's long-term value. The impact of this attributes to each generation contributing to the lasting value of OIs. For example, in many healthcare systems, the current Generation Z (Gen Z) workforce has already revolutionized the essence of OIs. As digital natives growing up in the Information Age, they have majorly influenced management styles of rapid, dynamic, progressive, and participative technological leadership. As a result, it has helped to accelerate the adoption of technology advancement in the modern workplace.

Using cutting-edge technologies provides assurance to patients, families, the workforce, and leaders to become digitally transformed and integrated into the healthcare system. This ensures that an organization can advance its processes by adopting a digital mindset. Broader innovative changes can then meet the ever-evolving needs of organizing people, patients, families, the workforce, and management.

Incorporating OIs while remaining committed to patient-centric approaches empowers healthcare providers to deliver the highest quality of care. This level of integration fosters an environment of continuous improvement and dedication to healthcare excellence, ensuring that the delivery of services not only meets but also exceeds patient expectations. These healthcare institutions can adapt to evolving patient needs, effectively integrate emerging health technologies, and maintain a focus on the quality and effectiveness of healthcare delivery services. The culmination of these efforts is a forward-thinking healthcare system that is both responsive and resilient, positioning itself at the forefront of medical innovation and patient satisfaction. Harmonizing strategic investment in advanced technology with the cultivation of a workforce skilled in future-ready competencies propels innovation and secures ongoing excellence in healthcare management. Designing and operating healthcare systems with a fundamental commitment to providing equitable healthcare services is crucial for attaining optimal health outcomes for all.

Farsighted, analytical, and proactive thinkers can envision the future beyond immediate challenges, embracing emerging trends and driving innovation to ensure a strong competitive edge. Farsighted leadership allows organizations to develop insights that are not limited to present conditions. It is arguably the most influential attribute in healthcare and serves as a beacon for insights within a healthcare organization. Such attributes look beyond immediate obstacles and anticipate future developments. The utmost diligence is necessary when it comes to selecting leaders for healthcare organizations, as there is a significant premium on insight at every level of healthcare leadership.

It is also important to discuss farsightedness in healthcare management, which involves a strategic approach to keeping an organization at the forefront of quality patient care, technological advancement, regulatory compliance, and efficient operations, all while being financially prudent. This perspective is essential for navigating the complexities of healthcare and delivering superior healthcare services. Farsightedness enriches OIs by extending their relevance into the future, ensuring an organization remains resilient and competitive.

Embracing the notion of timeless insight can be rewarding, as healthcare managers can promote this concept to help their organizations achieve a more efficient, effective, caring, and safe medical practices. This patient-centered approach should shape the evolution of a healthcare system, allowing it to become equitable, accountable, accessible, innovative, and sustainable with financial stability. These fundamentals are time-tested and have remained relevant through various phases of multiple leadership styles, regardless of period, place, circumstance, or context.

1.4 Insight Effects

An insight can be developed through an instinctive understanding of something, as opposed to an analytical perspective. This type of thought process comes down to the complexities of human cognition—especially in matters related to understanding insights and perception. As such, insights should be approached in a way that allows a future outcome to be shaped, as opposed to focusing solely on action. The objective of an insight effect is to eliminate an inflexible and myopic mindset that can obscure one's ability to make the best decisions or judgments. Insight, as a process, requires structured management through various schemes, which includes knowledge generation, information presentation, communication management, target audience analysis, team training, and sustainability and innovative growth.

Introducing the sciences of insight management has the potential to be revolutionary, as it can manage the way in which information flows through an organization to achieve positive results. This could involve the incorporation of specific educational programs from courses and workshops, along with graduate certificates as a tangible representation of such achievements. Optimization and adoption of OIs by an organization's senior management will undoubtedly achieve positive long-term results. However, OIs must be recognized as a profession that works within an organization's governance, with the objective of achieving widespread visibility and adoption.

The value of an insight effect is most apparent when determining its ability to propel an organization beyond preconceived boundaries and limitations. Having a bold insight challenges the status quo and helps inspire others to be more innovative, disruptive, and transformative. Moreover, by embracing bold insights, organizations can better differentiate themselves, seize new opportunities, and stay ahead of the competition in rapidly evolving markets. This approach encourages a culture that values experimentation, creativity, and risk-taking to move an organization toward long-term growth and success. Within this context, the "contemporary insight effect" can be defined as the transformative impact of gaining a fresh and relevant understanding of the current and rapidly changing market. It emphasizes the importance of staying abreast of current trends, technologies, and socioeconomic dynamics to extract valuable insights that drive organizational success.

When viewed from a contemporary context, where information is abundant and rapidly evolving, organizations must continuously work toward leveraging insights to remain competitive. The contemporary insight effect demands the timely identification of emerging opportunities, challenges, and market trends to guide organizations in making informed decisions, remaining innovative, and adapting their strategies to dynamically respond to evolving demands.

This effect underscores the significance of leveraging modern tools and methodologies, such as data analytics, artificial intelligence, and market research, to gain actionable insights that drive growth and foster resilience. By embracing the contemporary insight effect, organizations can position themselves for success in an ever-changing world. We are now more technologically connected than ever before, and the social media age has given us access to unprecedented amounts of information. However, with this abundance of data, there needs to be precision of insight. In other words, the ability to translate data into actionable insights through context-driven decisions is crucial.

Regarding the healthcare industry, the addition of online insights to the strategy of insight management creates the most responsive opportunity for the standardized gathering and analysis of patient's preferences, concerns, and behaviors. Quasi-insights can be extremely relevant to healthcare insight management. It will therefore likely help towards assessing and validating the implementation of actionable insights.

1.5 Insight Content

It is important for OIs to be well established, managed, developed, and sustained. When looking into the operations of any organization, insights serve as powerful and effective tools that facilitate uniqueness, strength, survival, visibility, optimization, planning, and sustainability. In short, organizational content is crucial for insight management. On the topic of content, it is necessary to create something that contributes and delivers to OIs, which can be achieved by a narrative consisting of vision, engagement, differentiation, resourcefulness, priority iteration, aspiration, and inspiring innovation. Ensuring that a narrative remains relevant and dynamic is a challenging prospect. Therefore, building an evolving narrative over time is the central premise for insight management. An enduring narrative that leads to lasting experiences, influence, and professionalism can be developed and communicated through conventional channels such as social interaction, event participation, print channels, and broadcast media; modern platforms such as social media, vlogging, direct messaging, tweets, and user-generated content; and transmedia, which utilizes both conventional and modern methods.

1.6 The Delphi Method and Insights

The Delphi method (or Delphi technique) is a research tool that adopts a structured approach to gathering and synthesizing expert opinions to make informed decisions and predictions. This method relies on expert knowledge and opinions through surveys that provide feedback and iteration for contented decisions. It is often described as a collective database of intelligence and wisdom and is expertized for the purpose of providing a systematic approach. Hence, this method can generate invaluable information for content while also presenting a strategic direction with an agreed roadmap from internal and external experts of various backgrounds. As an example, a study conducted at Johns Hopkins Hospital utilized a modified Delphi approach to align critical care interventions with patient goals. The study convened a panel of experts, including critical care physicians, ICU nurses, former ICU patients, and family members. Over three rounds of surveys, the panel identified eight non-emergent interventions commonly performed in intensive care units that could be potentially harmful and require a clear understanding of patients' treatment goals. This consensus-driven process underscored the importance of shared decision-making in critical care settings, demonstrating how the Delphi method can effectively harness collective expertise to address complex healthcare challenges and improve patient safety protocols (Turnbull et al., 2016).

The value of the Delphi method also lies in its ability to generate meta insights, providing organizations with a solid foundation for future business decisions. For instance, healthcare organizations can become better prepared for transformative technology, enabling a pathway for new innovations such as appropriateness methods and an expert lens that contains an enhanced but traditional version of the original Delphi process. In view of this, a recent study employed a global Delphi consensus process to develop an Emergency Department Safety Checklist aimed at reducing medical errors. This collaborative effort resulted in a comprehensive safety checklist tailored for emergency department settings, offering a structured framework to monitor and enhance patient safety during emergency care (Rovati et al., 2024). Furthermore, it can be used as a foresight tool to identify emerging technology and innovative change models in healthcare. Böhmdorfer-McNair et al. (2021) developed and applied a modified Delphi method to assess medication safety in an Austrian level II hospital. This structured approach facilitated a comprehensive evaluation of the hospital's medication safety practices, identifying improvement areas, and providing a reproducible method for synthesizing expert opinions on medication safety (Böhmdorfer-McNair et al., 2021). In addition, the Delphi method can be used as a tool to anticipate, forecast, and prepare for upcoming and evolving opportunities and risks. A 2017 study employed the Delphi method to identify human factors associated with nursing errors, revealing critical causes such as heavy workload and fatigue. This consensus-driven approach provided a foundation for anticipating and developing strategies to mitigate nursing errors and improve patient safety in hospital settings (Roth et al., 2017). Similarly, a recent study conducted in Saudi Arabia utilized a three-round Delphi process to achieve consensus on the essential skills and knowledge for effective virtual healthcare delivery. The study engaged a panel of experts, including policymakers, healthcare professionals, academicians, and telehealth specialists, who identified 151 competencies across 33 domains, with prominent domains being communication, professionalism, leadership, health informatics, digital literacy, and clinical expertise. This framework provided a foundation for training programs, enabling healthcare professionals to be well-equipped to deliver high-quality virtual care (Al Baalharith & Aboshaiqah, 2024). Adopting this type of proactive insight development and management can be novel, game-changing, and disruptive while also offering breakthroughs or bundles. A 2019 study employed a modified Delphi approach to explore the key factors that influence the implementation of government-directed policies within hospital settings. The researchers engaged 11 international experts with extensive experience in policy development and implementation across various health systems. Through iterative survey rounds, the panel reached consensus on 24 key factors deemed important for policy implementation. However, only 20 of these factors were considered feasible for practical application, which underscores the utility of the Delphi method in implementing government-directed policies in hospitals (Havers et al., 2019). In short, Delphi insights consist of valuable information, prediction, and recommendation tools that enable organizations to reach consensus through a diverse network of experts and stakeholders.

1.7 Conspicuous Insights

These are instinctive observations or realizations that are knowledgeably visible and noticeable. When insights are conspicuous, they are clear and prominent, though often subconscious, concreate, and accurate. While there isn't a specific, widely recognized theory called "Conspicuous Insights Theory" in healthcare management, it can be constructed as a strategic approach focusing on the identification and application of key insights that stand out due to their potential to drive substantial improvements in healthcare systems.

The Conspicuous Framework for Organizational Insights posits a framework through which leadership insights impact organizational outcomes, particularly in the healthcare sector where quality, safety, and efficiency are closely tied to leadership and strategic choices. This framework delineates how two principal categories of factors—leaders' characteristics and external forces—shape key organizational dynamics and image, ultimately influencing the overall insights.

Among the key leaders' characteristics, experience and education form the backbone of their decision-making capabilities. Healthcare leaders with robust clinical backgrounds, along with management education navigate, both medical complexities and operational challenges easily. Research indicates that leadership interventions in healthcare settings can improve healthcare outcomes by approximately **14%**, thus highlighting the critical impact of effective leadership (Restivo et al., 2022). Beyond formal qualifications, compassion, effective problem-solving, intuition, and self-discipline represent essential qualities for healthcare leaders, enabling them to build meaningful relationships and address challenges ranging from budget management to complex patient care issues.

The healthcare sector faces rigorous regulatory frameworks that substantially impact operational decisions. Research indicates that regulatory changes can create substantial administrative burdens for healthcare providers, potentially affecting their ability to deliver timely care (Mosadeghrad, 2014). For example, when new patient privacy regulations are implemented, healthcare organizations must invest in training, technology, and process redesign to ensure compliance. Effective leaders recognize these regulatory shifts early and position their organizations to adapt efficiently. In addition, financial stability is one of the key external factors that significantly affect organizational strategy and performance.

The interaction between leadership characteristics and external forces manifests through the conspicuous factors that directly influence organizational performance. Among them, the organizational culture represents the most pervasive conspicuous factor, shaping employee behavior, patient experience, and operational efficiency. Research demonstrates that organizational culture significantly impacts healthcare professionals' performance when mediated by work discipline (Almutairi et al., 2022). Furthermore, employee engagement also plays a crucial role, with research indicating that healthcare organizations with engaged employees experience lower turnover rates, fewer medical errors, and higher patient satisfaction scores (Janes et al., 2021). In addition, digital transformation has become a cornerstone of innovation and efficiency in healthcare. Organizations that effectively implement technological solutions can revolutionize their operations, enhance patient care, and streamline core processes. For example, Mayo Clinic partnered with Google Cloud to integrate AI into its electronic health record (EHR) system, utilizing natural language processing (NLP) and predictive analytics to improve clinical decision-making and reduce the administrative burdens. This innovation helped in reduced manual data entry, improved diagnostic precision, and prompt identification of patients at risk for severe conditions (Series et al., 2022).

The combined influence of leader characteristics and external forces directly contributes to key organizational outcomes. Among the few, patient outcomes depict the ultimate measure of healthcare effectiveness (Fig. 1.1). Organizations that excel in the conspicuous factors (visionary leadership, for instance) typically exhibit superior clinical outcomes and better patient satisfaction scores. For example, when patients are satisfied, they are more likely to adhere to treatment plans, return for follow-up care, and recommend the organization to others. Additionally, healthcare professionals in such environments report higher job satisfaction and lower burnout, which further enhances care quality and continuity. Finally, organizations that successfully navigate leadership and external demands tend to achieve better revenue and sustainability, enabling long-term investments in infrastructure as well as human resources.

In essence, the Conspicuous Framework of Organizational Insights underscores the pivotal role of leaders in navigating both intrinsic personal capabilities and extrinsic environmental pressures to foster an organizational culture that promotes high performance, excellence, resilience, and sustainable outcomes. Leaders who score high on conspicuous factors not only enhance operational efficiencies but also contribute significantly to the well-being of their patients and the broader community they serve. Thus, they become crucial in achieving superior healthcare institutions (Fig. 1.1).

1.8 Five Powerful Methods for Growth and Innovation

To achieve the highest level of success in an organization, one should look no further than the power of the following five approaches: insight effects, online insights, quasi-insights, Delphi insights, and meta insights. To create a culture with a shared platform that seeks to achieve ambitious goals, synergy and alignment must be attained on an individual and collective level. Applying the aforementioned approaches sets up an organization in the best way possible to achieve such goals.

These five methods are better defined as:

1. Insight Effects

   The transformative impact of gaining a fresh and relevant understanding of the current and rapidly changing market to drive organizational success.
2. Online Insights

   Gathering and analyzing digital data, such as social media and online behavior, to understand trends, preferences, and engagement.

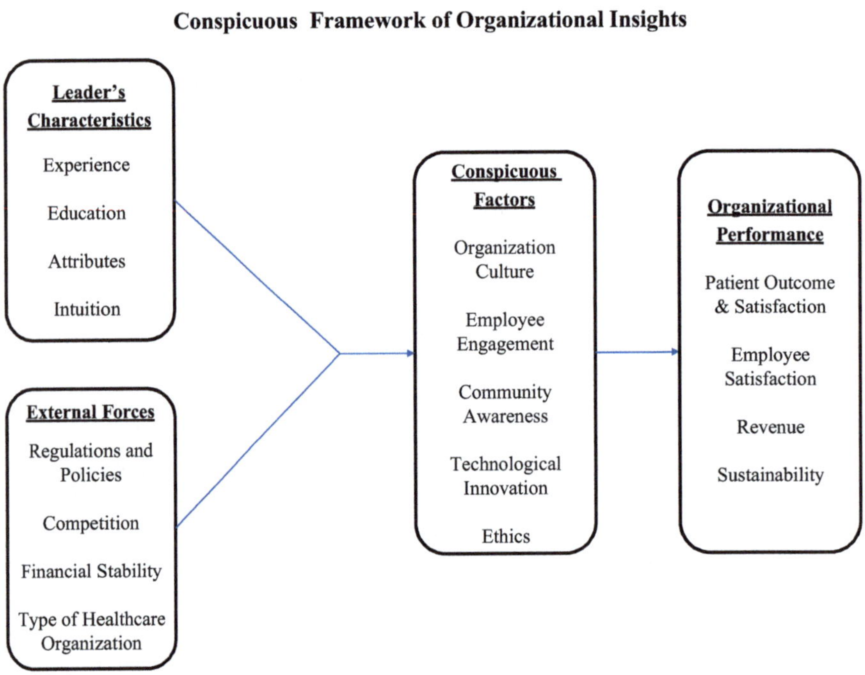

Fig. 1.1 Conspicuous Framework of Organizational Insights. Note: Indeed (2025). 12 Characteristics for Effective Leadership in Healthcare. Accessed from https://www.indeed.com/career-advice/career-development/leadership-in-healthcare

3. Quasi-Insights

   Preliminary or partial insights that are developed through limited data and analysis, often serving as a basis for further investigation and validation.
4. Delphi Insights

   Insights generated through the Delphi method, which involves gathering expert opinions through surveys to make informed decisions and predictions.
5. Meta Insights

   Comprehensive insights that integrate and synthesize findings from multiple sources and methods to provide a broader understanding and strategic direction.

References

Al Baalharith, I. M., & Aboshaiqah, A. E. (2024, March). A Delphi study on identifying competencies in virtual healthcare for healthcare professionals. In *Healthcare* (Vol. 12, No. 7, p. 739). MDPI.

Almutairi, R., Aditya, R. S., Kodriyah, L., Yusuf, A., Solikhah, F. K., Al Razeeni, D. M., et al. (2022). Analysis of organizational culture factors that influence the performance of health care professionals: A literature review. *Journal of Public Health in Africa, 13*(Suppl 2), 2415.

Böhmdorfer-McNair, B., Huf, W., Strametz, R., Nebosis, M., Pichler, F., Janowitz, S. M., et al. (2021). Finding consensus about the level of medication safety in a hospital setting: development and an example of application of a modified Delphi method. *Frontiers in Public Health, 9*, 630398.

Havers, S. M., Martin, E., Wilson, A., & Hall, L. (2019). Implementation of government-directed policy in the hospital setting: A modified Delphi study. *Health Research Policy and Systems, 17*, 1–10.

Indeed. (2025). 12 characteristics for effective leadership in healthcare. Accessed from https://www.indeed.com/career-advice/career-development/leadership-in-healthcare

Janes, G., Mills, T., Budworth, L., Johnson, J., & Lawton, R. (2021). The association between health care staff engagement and patient safety outcomes: A systematic review and meta-analysis. *Journal of Patient Safety, 17*(3), 207–216.

Mosadeghrad, A. M. (2014). Factors affecting medical service quality. *Iranian Journal of Public Health, 43*(2), 210.

Restivo, V., Minutolo, G., Battaglini, A., Carli, A., Capraro, M., Gaeta, M., et al. (2022). Leadership effectiveness in healthcare settings: A systematic review and meta-analysis of cross-sectional and before–after studies. *International Journal of Environmental Research and Public Health, 19*(17), 10995.

Roth, C., Brewer, M., & Wieck, K. L. (2017, July). Using a Delphi method to identify human factors contributing to nursing errors. In *Nursing forum* (Vol. 52, No. 3, pp. 173–179).

Rovati, L., Privitera, D., Finch, A. S., Litell, J,M,, Brogan, A.M., Tekin, A., et al. (2024). Development of an emergency department safety checklist through a global consensus process. *Internal and Emergency Medicine*. https://doi.org/10.1007/s11739-024-03760-y

Series, T. L. H. S., Grossmann, C., Chua, P. S., Ahmed, M., & Greene, S. M. (2022). Case study: Mayo-Google partnership. In *Sharing health data: The why, the will, and the way forward.* National Academies Press.

Turnbull, A. E., Sahetya, S. K., & Needham, D. M. (2016). Aligning critical care interventions with patient goals: A modified Delphi study. *Heart and Lung: Journal of Acute and Critical Care, 45*(6), 517–524. https://doi.org/10.1016/j.hrtlng.2016.07.011

Digital Insights

2

Karine Sargsyan

The medical field in general, particularly medical science and contemporary healthcare, is rapidly evolving globally. The fulminant developments in the general IT sector and the application of digital tools for medicine, in particular, have been increasing in the last decades worldwide, with overflowing developments over the previous 4–5 years. This extraordinary growth can contribute to patients' changing needs (patient-facing applications to human-facing applications like 23andMe) and a stringent need to enhance operational efficiencies in the healthcare sector. The newest IT tools in healthcare are supporting innovation dually: a) to enhance efficiency and b) to deliver IT-powered healthcare services (Haleem et al., 2022; Krishnamoorthy et al., 2023). The described developments have considerable potential to enhance medical outcomes. Medical/healthcare professionals support these technologies, revolutionizing patient care and improving healthcare outcomes and experiences (Awad et al., 2021; Massaro, 2023). Different technologies that can interoperate and communicate their data seamlessly are being developed to facilitate collaborative care and better healthcare quality (Marques & Ferreira, 2020). Beyond that, introducing electronic communication systems in the care delivery system and beyond will bring considerable overhauls in access to and quality of healthcare. With modern large-scale electronic systems and communication gadgets, online access to healthcare services for the general public and patients is believed to improve, especially in remote populations and underserved communities. This can revolutionize healthcare delivery by bridging geographical barriers

K. Sargsyan (✉)
IBD Institute and OncoBiobank, Cedars-Sinai Medical Center, Los Angeles, CA, USA

International Biobanking and Education, Medical University of Graz, Graz, Austria

Department of Digital Medicine and AI and Department of Medical Genetics, Yerevan State Medical University, Yerevan, Armenia
e-mail: Karine.Sargsyan@cshs.org

B. Alknawy (ed.), *Organizational Insights: Healthcare Perspective*, Springer Series in Healthcare Management and Innovation,
https://doi.org/10.1007/978-3-032-10532-5_2

among health professionals and bringing their expertise in real time (Sheikh et al., 2021). There is an intrinsic power of transformative change in Health IT through the manifolds times increase in the rate of translation of medical evidence into practice, keeping health providers at the doorstep of the latest developments in their field. This brings evidence-based medicine and technology together and compels them to challenge each other even further, leading to optimal care—tailored care based on high-quality clinical evidence. Ignorantly or otherwise, there is much more to be discovered on how best to utilize the health facilities of poor pockets and far-flung rural communities. It can be the number one tool revolutionizing healthcare provision by bridging distances so that health professionals can share their expertise in real time (Mbunge et al., 2021). Health IT is driving a very substantial change and significantly increases the translation rate of medical evidence into practice, thus enabling health providers. Indeed, the dynamic integration of technology with evidence-based medicine can provide optimum patient care based on patients' needs, backed by robust clinical evidence. It is, however, proper to point out that the best way to use the capabilities of health IT toward these ends remains largely under exploration (Marques & Ferreira, 2020; Budd et al. 2020). Furthermore, the historical development of digital technologies in healthcare shows a clear, constant upward trajectory driven by both the changing needs of patients and the need for enhanced efficiency and effectiveness within this sector. Health IT can dramatically advance medical outcomes through collaborative care and innovation in healthcare delivery. It is an investment in research and development; these technologies have real potential to shape optimal patient care and further transform healthcare. Such growth in these digital technologies for health holds the opportunity to bridge gaps in healthcare access, particularly for the most marginalized communities and those living in remote areas (Yao et al., 2022). Healthcare experts are already extending their reach and providing top-notch care to people without access to healthcare. Without technology, they would probably have faced significant barriers to care. Besides, artificial intelligence and machine learning significantly enhance how health providers analyze medical data for proper diagnosis and personalized treatment. As Barrett and Orlikowski stated in 2021, big data analytics integrated with predictive modelling helps healthcare institutions proactively identify and address population health challenges to improve health outcomes and cost savings. The future of healthcare majorly depends on the continued development of digital technology, as it contributes massively to transforming healthcare and the patient/healthy population experience, ultimately improving people's quality of life (Barrett & Orlikowski, 2021). The use of modern technologies (not only digital ones) in healthcare worldwide is dramatically increasing, and the recent technological breakthroughs are influencing this trend even more. This breathtaking progress can be attributed mainly to patients' changing needs and expectations and the pressing necessity of optimizing operational efficiencies within the healthcare sector. Therefore, the pursuit of IT healthcare innovation will primarily be driven by the dual objectives of attaining higher efficiency and effectiveness in delivering and managing health services. The substantial potential of health information technologies to improve medical outcomes is a powerful impetus for this continuing change in healthcare (Chandra et al., 2022). Optimism and faith in the huge potential of these technologies in changing healthcare for the better—at least, improvement in healthcare outcomes and experience—are shared and firmly held. However, vigorous work is being done to create an atmosphere for appropriate sharing and exchange of data across different technologies. At the same time, the ultimate vision remains to enable collaborative care and support quality in healthcare services. Besides that, the wide adoption of electronic communication systems within the care delivery system and beyond can potentially change access to quality healthcare services. Electronic communication could improve access to health services, particularly for remote populations and underserved communities. More than that, it can revolutionize healthcare delivery and break geographical barriers for health professionals who can use their skill sets more appropriately in real time (Cordeiro, 2021). Health IT has a place in turning this evidence into action at unprecedented rates and provides health professionals with an understanding of current trends in their field. This dynamic coupling of technology and evidence-based medicine will ensure that the best possible treatment, patient-variant as it is, based on a robust underlying clinical rationale, is delivered. There are plenty of areas to assess and strategize how to implement health IT to provide the best healthcare service. The trajectory of digital technologies in health remains a constant upslope due to the ever-evolving nature of patient needs and the critical call for enhancing efficiency and effectiveness within the industry. It holds immense promise to improve medical outcomes and collaboration by changing how healthcare is delivered and revolutionizing healthcare delivery (Golinelli et al., 2020). As their potential unravels, so does the need for investment in robust research and development and capitalizing on their capabilities for optimal healthcare for patients and remodeling healthcare. The growth of these healthcare-based digital technologies allows the opportunity to fill all the gaps in healthcare access, particularly among the marginalized population living in remote areas. With the complete potential of telemedicine and remote patient monitoring, care professionals are empowered to provide high-quality healthcare to those who otherwise face numerous problems receiving health-related services. The conscious development of AI and ML technologies for medicine and in the scope of healthcare continues to revolutionize how health providers analyze and interpret medical data for more precise diagnoses and develop personalized treatment plans. With the integration of predictive modeling and big data, healthcare organizations can forecast population health status more accurately and take timely action without bearing additional costs. The future of medicine and healthcare emerges in the sustained expansion and consummate application of digital technologies because they bear undisputed potential for changing how healthcare is delivered and experienced, contributing to the overall betterment of individuals' lives both locally and globally (Dang et al., 2020).

2.1 Leveraging Technology in Healthcare

This comparative assessment gives critical insights to policymakers and healthcare stakeholders as they strive to deliver optimum healthcare to their respective populations. Through these kinds of constant and relentless efforts, it finally becomes increasingly possible to identify emerging trends, innovative approaches, and evidence-based strategies for sharing with health professionals across the globe. In shared work and idea-sharing, we can strive for better quality in a changing healthcare landscape, bringing about better patient outcomes and improved health at a population level (Trout et al., 2022). Since IT is rapidly changing, its influence on healthcare quality must be properly assessed and monitored for the benefits and challenges it presents. Through the assistance of health systems technology in the coming future, we can use it to model best practices so that it will fulfill its function of improving population health without being associated with adverse side effects. With continuous vigilance and adaptability, we can tap into the full power of technology to ultimately revolutionize and advance healthcare delivery across the globe (Sipanoun et al., 2022). Besides the points mentioned above, there needs to be collaboration among policymakers, healthcare stakeholders, and researchers or data analysts in data collection and interpretation. This fosters a better comprehension of healthcare needs, proper resource allocation, and the possibility of identifying areas for improvement. The insights learned from the power of data will inform policymakers and other health stakeholders to make appropriate decisions, undertake proper interventions, and bring about change to improve population health outcomes. Another important development to remember is that it is essential to recognize the increasing role in healthcare delivery and care. Outcome improvement is greatly embedded in empowering patients and individuals to participate actively in their healthcare (Manias et al., 2020). We can work towards creating a collaborative environment between the healthcare provider and the patient by promoting patient education, shared decision-making, and access to personal health information. A system like this is more satisfying for patients, greatly improves patient satisfaction, and enhances health outcomes while reducing healthcare costs (Nijor et al., 2022). As we increase technology usage in healthcare, some challenges and considerations must be thoroughly investigated. Health information should be prioritized for patients' privacy on issues concerning confidentiality and security. Stringent measures that ensure robust protection of data protection through strict regulations could reduce such breaches and unauthorized access. Health professionals should also learn many skills and get training to use and leverage technology effectively in their practice (Trout et al., 2022). Continuous professional development and education programs should be implemented to ensure adequate skilling of health professionals on the potential use of technologies. The conclusion is that this detailed review and other prior recommendations provide depth of insight and value to policy decision-makers and healthcare stakeholders to optimize and maximize healthcare delivery. By embracing and capitalizing on new emerging trends, leveraging the immeasurable power and potential of technology, engaging the active participation of patients, and engaging in efforts to surmount a range of diverse challenges, we have an outstanding opportunity to inspire innovation and progress in healthcare delivery worldwide (Sipanoun et al., 2022). With enhanced collaboration and adoption of evidence-based strategies, including the integration of data-driven decision-making processes, we can significantly advance the health of populations, drive better patient outcomes, and ultimately bring into existence a more efficient, effective, and patient-centered healthcare and medical system addressing the various needs of persons and communities at large around the world. Traditionally, analysis in healthcare systems used to be time-consuming, with very minimal results. Clinical outcome evidence has been elusive, and the morbidity of patients' health status is only appreciated after many years of observation and data collection. However, because of the new healthcare technology innovations, the availability and accessibility of and to patients' information in electronic medical records and inpatient monitoring systems have grown exponentially. Availability and access to enhanced patient information have reached an unprecedented level. However, even with all this patient information, we continue to grapple with being able to turn it into something meaningful and helpful (Manias et al., 2020). Further ahead, one can look at the actual impact of information technology on healthcare quality by reviewing or considering the Advanced Information Management (AIM) Program adopted for implementation in both the Cleveland Department of Veterans Affairs and the University Hospitals of Cleveland. It is a very typical example of how IT can be integrated effectively into the medical environment and used in healthcare. However, it also provides much insight into how it could benefit patients and healthcare service providers. As advanced, are information management systems incorporated into our healthcare system as they allow for streamlining data collection, analysis, and reporting? This is leading to better decision-making and higher quality of patient care. The vision and actual application of information technology in healthcare systems are the motivators for future growth and evolution. With technology, we are transforming healthcare delivery by optimizing medical processes and diagnostic decisions, bringing better clinical outcomes and our dream of a far more inclusive, patient-centric, and efficient healthcare system for all into reality (Nijor et al., 2022).

2.2 Addressing Challenges in Digital Healthcare Transformation

2.2.1 Key Challenges in Digital Healthcare Transformation

Digital technology and its implementation in the existing health system have been a constant process since its creation, and it is developing parallel to the technological development of IT systems as well as diagnostic and therapeutic methods and machines in the healthcare industry. More and more patient information is being kept in silico, and cybersecurity is becoming a serious issue in this industry (Barbazzeni et al., 2022). The COVID-19 pandemic has driven the development of telehealth services for recording patient information online and has shown the need for the process of cloud computing-compliant with the regulations in each country but also internationally (as a network of health delivery across the whole globe)—in a secure environment under the scope of a single healthcare provider. Apart from telehealth or telemedicine, there has also been a wearable technology explosion and another direct patient requirement to further guarantee the collection and storage of this new data recording securely and still well usable in health practice. The creation of an elastic and dynamic cloud-based, cyber-secured platform for the secure storage, analysis, and retrieval of patient data, in full accordance with the ISO/IEC 27000 standards as well as the GDPR and NIH regulations, at the basis of a vast number of new products and services, is becoming more challenging every day (Maleka & Matli, 2024).

On the other hand, the era of digital invoicing is an evolutionary phase with the introduction of smart contracts, blockchain, and emerging payment technology to revolutionize the verification of services and settlements. Convergence can ensure control and transparency in professional services as the digital invoice is implemented. Healthcare price transparency remains essential to patients and the system, allowing patients to make informed decisions on care providers as a function of treatment cost dynamics. Mobile apps and internet-based repositories of healthcare products facilitate an easy comparison of diagnostic and treatment products. Customers can retrieve a product's in-depth cost, usage history, and cost cover (Lin et al., 2025). Improving the patient experience is at the core, accompanied by sustainable health innovation and business strategy. The new technology system aims to revolutionize healthcare with a patient-centric model focusing on prevention rather than just treatment. It helps reduce costs by initially healing diseases presymptomatically, which may lead to a reimbursement process for the patient and lower costs for the system. Integrated mobile applications developed for diet consumption tracking and meal planning also suggest healthy meal recipes according to requirements (Pulimamidi, 2024).

2.2.2 Technological Barriers

Redesigning healthcare services concerning digital technologies offers the potential to introduce innovative and novel e-health solutions with expansion and personalization potential for prevention. The redesign of medical services due to the impact of digital technologies also translates into a colossal number of technological, legal, ethical, social, and organizational issues (Stefanicka-Wojtas & Kurpas, 2022). The challenges necessitate action from different stakeholders, such as medical and non-medical personnel, the government, non-governmental institutions and businesses, and academic bodies.

Electronic health services (eHealth) and mobile health services (mHealth) are changing the healthcare scenario by giving patients autonomy to control the treatment process. This is achievable through integrating medical data to enable the provision of relevant medical decisions to medical practitioners. Legal paperwork and records now present challenges in seeking access to critical information, and there must be a strong infrastructure that integrates data onto numerous devices and involves new tech like artificial intelligence but also covers all security issues in analysis (Spinean et al., 2024). A communications platform for collecting eHealth databases and interoperable devices should be guaranteed to the population. eHealth system development requires innovative cross-platform authentication, standards of data exchange, and overall chronic disease models. With the eHealth revolution, contemporary medical services should be by legal requirements of quality, safety, and full rights for service recipients. This revolutionary change of advanced medical treatment raised to e-health, which enhanced patient involvement and re-engineered healthcare delivery in the information era (Crispo et al., 2024).

2.2.3 Regulatory and Compliance Issues

With the computerization of the health process and system becoming a formal objective of most countries in the world, pressure has mounted to understand the requirements of the healthcare sector in order to be ready for the adjournment. There are a few questions regarding restructuring and how to do this. Now that it has been signed into law, the PPACA has generated infinite administrative, judicial, legislative, and ethical resistance. The President has needed to come to the defense of the Act and its purposes, and Congress and the Senate have challenged each other to act against it (Miller & Payne, 2016).

Once the patient has an appointment and, after discharge from the hospital, the patient can purchase a collection of medical records. The astronomically high processing charges requested for copies of the records or their reproductions have infuriated patients and other physicians contemplating treating and diagnosing simply from having constant, easily accessible access to the papers. For example, the Indian healthcare system is highly burdened, and the key reasons for this are inflated insurance claims and gross misdiagnosis cases. The most significant contributory cause is inadequate patient medical histories. Electronic health records are a considerable revolution that provides healthcare personnel with the authority to observe and treat patients with ease. However, it has put substantial stress on the health infrastructure to properly sort the patients' records while maintaining confidentiality (Miller & Payne, 2016; Hamid et al., 2024).

Once the patient has an appointment, and after discharge from the hospital, the patient can purchase a collection of medical records. The astronomically high processing charges requested for copies of the records or their reproductions have infuriated patients and other physicians contemplating treating and diagnosing simply from having constant, easily accessible access to the papers. For example, the Indian healthcare system is highly burdened, and the key reasons for this are inflated insurance claims and gross misdiagnosis cases. The most significant contributory cause is inadequate patient medical histories. Electronic health records are a considerable revolution that provides healthcare personnel with the authority to observe and treat patients with ease. However, it has put substantial stress on the health infrastructure to properly sort the patients' records while maintaining confidentiality (Hamid et al., 2024).

As patients increasingly demand their medical records, healthcare transparency is on the agenda. This being considered, and with budgetary pressures, U.S. legislators have held hearings to review the matters. The HITECH Act hearings—enacted into law in 2009 to further protect patient information—centered on simplifying health information exchange procedures. Before the widespread use of electronic records, confidentiality breaches were typically one-time, incidental occurrences because of uncomplicated strategies. Pre-HIPAA days lacked sufficient regulations to protect patient privacy for medical data, with malicious users often relying on social engineering to exploit human vulnerabilities and extract sensitive data (Janarthanan et al., 2024).

2.2.4 Cultural Resistance

The development of the whole medical industry and large-scale business, in general, is immediately relevant to technological innovation and virtual transformation, which will naturally enhance the provision and organization of medical care. However, that kind of transformation has its burdens; for example, it tends to provoke opposition from employees who must implement it.

This study investigates how technological advancements in healthcare influence employee resistance in three case studies: digitalization of patient records, reporting adverse events, and digital signatures for patient information management. Key sources of resistance are shaped significantly by the healthcare culture, employees' attitudes, and responses to new technology. This evolutionary process results in a visible resistance to change due to ingrained assumptions about best practices. Healthcare managers face the challenge of introducing innovations to enhance care delivery (Sharma & Joshi, 2021).

By examining the literature, we see that practices needed to enact cultural transformation with large campus building projects, suggesting that such projects could be coordinated for shared benefits, leading to a model of effective managerial practices. Despite the benefits of digital technologies, their adoption is challenging. Physicians are also concerned that increasingly sophisticated systems will further erode the physician-patient relationship and that more must be coddled to facilitate face-to-face communication. New technologies, such as camera sensors and mixed-reality displays, are suggested to continue building patient-physician rapport within an exam environment. The literature shows the technology's work of contributing to the development of the sense of knowledge, confidence, empathy, and a sense of care in particular, thereby blending and further integrating the experience of the encounter with a patient (Wu et al., 2022).

2.2.5 Data Security and Privacy Concerns

Internet (or so-called distance) medicine will have a lot to do with all ages and capabilities, but future care home services will only be able to offer meals and essential living support. Healthcare will be vastly different in the next 30 years in the aging network. Detailed online systems with enormous databases of drug research, symptom comparison, CPR maintenance assistance, family alert services, and more will be available for government and private agencies. All these technologies can form one image of high-tech care, which will become out of reach for the majority by the time 2050 arrives (Landesz et al., 2023). Several digital health aid programs are being designed to fulfill such needs. Non-invasive healthcare monitoring through innovative technology and building a software platform for easy integration are underway. Future wireless memory networks will further the intelligent delivery of care at a point of health change. The Health Insurance Portability and Accountability Act (HIPAA) and the Federal Information Security Management Act (FISMA) became laws to protect sensitive information in government agencies and the confidentiality of patients. Hospitals need to implement safe management of data and legal requirements. However, with technologies like Bring Your Own Devices (BYOD), mobile technology, instant messaging, and cloud computing, new security threats have emerged. With the Internet of Things (IoT), it is more challenging to maintain data privacy because healthcare professionals and facilities are often unaware of these threats. Healthcare systems online today must bear patients' confidential data. Problems caused by BYOD, cell phones, and instant messaging by healthcare staff, as well as how patient privacy is maintained, are covered. Data security controls and data compliance with FISMA and HIPAA regulations are explained (Ahmed, 2019).

2.3 Strategies for Successful Transformation

Managers fixate on regulation and expense and forget about industry change and strategy. Curing and treating pandemics, governments, insurers, health, medical services, patients, and technology are hard to piece together. In this one-sided business world, attention is an expensive commodity. There are no clear guides or wisdom to adhere to and refer to, and resistance to change easily comes without a wide-angle vision. Testing programs provide those most impacted by them with a clearer view and some breathing space amidst cost and compliance issues. Organizations can discover and overcome minor differences in their context over time. These programs allow organizations to observe how they fit in between disrupting trends to have a genuine picture of external capabilities. An awareness of potential disruptions below the surface allows for an opportunity for a specific response to facilitate changes in roles, structures, processes, and services to drive positive disruptions throughout industries (Wu et al., 2022).

2.3.1 Change Management Approaches

Internet (or so-called distance) medicine will have a lot to do with all ages and capabilities, but future care home services will only be able to offer meals and essential living support. Healthcare will be vastly different in the next 30 years in the aging network. Detailed online systems with enormous databases of drug research, symptom comparison, CPR maintenance assistance, family alert services, and more will be available for government and private agencies. All these technologies can form one image of high-tech care, which will become out of reach for the majority by the time 2050 arrives (Landesz et al., 2023). Several digital health aid programs are being designed to fulfill such needs. Non-invasive healthcare monitoring through innovative technology and building a software platform for easy integration are underway. Future wireless memory networks will further the intelligent delivery of care at a point of health change. The Health Insurance Portability and Accountability Act (HIPAA) and the Federal Information Security Management Act (FISMA) became laws to protect sensitive information in government agencies and the confidentiality of patients (Goffman & Glatstein, 2004). Hospitals need to implement safe management of data and legal requirements. However, with technologies like Bring Your Own Devices (BYOD), mobile technology, instant messaging, and cloud computing, there are new security threats. With the Internet of Things (IoT), it is more challenging to maintain data privacy because healthcare professionals and facilities are unaware of these threats. Healthcare systems online today must bear patients' confidential data. Problems caused by BYOD, cell phones, and instant messaging by healthcare staff, as well as how patient privacy is maintained, are covered. Data security controls and data compliance with FISMA and HIPAA regulations are explained (Naib et al., 2024).

2.3.2 Lessons Learned from Failure

Faster development of software health creates credibility and success issues, which need to be criticized occasionally by the Digital Health Initiative (DHTI) if the latter has to be credible. Investment only has software health business proposals with trial periods, with software underjoining careful assessment and criticism that must be incorporated. DHTI has managed to deploy digital solutions to real healthcare needs and has compiled significant learnings. Adapting principles like scientific rigor and process standardization by DHTI lies at the center of the appeal for digital technology to change the face of healthcare. Healthcare organizations have to keep pace with the technology to be in line with society's behavioral change, and there is a direct impact on service delivery, with digital natives being new healthcare consumers. The DHTI ignites a digital revolution in children's and youth's health and well-being, promoting quality, value, and equity through harnessing digital capital (Alzghaibi, 2023; Hourani et al., 2021).

2.3.3 Ethical Issues

Emerging incredibly rapidly, digital health technologies, specifically ML and AI applications, offer new and powerful tools for biomedical research, disease prevention, and healthcare delivery. They pose new ethical and regulatory challenges at the same time. Current analyses by privacy experts frequently do not address regulatory- and ethical-privacy-management-specific issues of new technologies or record obstacles to effective privacy management due to a lack of tools, standards, or familiarity with best practices. A tailored and actionable R&CT tool would enable research teams, institutional review boards (IRBs), and regulators overseeing such research to more effectively handle and appreciate emerging technologies' harms and potential harms and build stronger protections for participants. Such tools could stop research from entering the highly regulated health data zone. Today, if ever, is the time for technology developers, the research community, policymakers, and funding agencies to recognize and act on anticipated future ethical, privacy, and regulatory concerns regarding emerging technologies to use in healthcare and digital health research (Nebeker et al., 2019).

A brief presentation by a physician and information scientist is followed by an abstract of ethics questions that arose when a presentation on decision-making by a statistician in research on patient drug choice elicited a reaction from an E-health medical historian. Whether aspects of the contribution of digital technology would eventually preclude decision-making on medical evidence from being distinctive, equal, secure, and transparent, as required for validity, was questioned. The argument in the discussion after the presentation puts an IRB, a Patient Organization, and a government DE before the speaker. These indicate some of the serious challenges for medical informatics: how to construct ethical criteria for the freedom of choice in disease choice sets, therapy choice sets, and health promotion choice sets, and how to construct protection strategies from an accurate understanding of the quality and type of information adequate for various communities. The corrective measures of scientific evidence for the outcomes are very complex, and their comparison relies on a shared language, which in most instances does not exist even among professional medical communities (Kulikowski, 2022).

2.3.4 Informed Consent in Digital Interventions

While overall broadband access has been better in recent years, let us not forget that many individuals cannot access it or engage digitally. Some provisions must be made to see that, besides digital solutions, such groups are catered to, and measures to offset the digital divide exist (Teare et al., 2020). I suggest that DC place such groups in the limelight. So far, DC has been employed in the context of questions to be ostensibly posed by a more active population of research activity or at least a more active population of Internet activity. Examples of questions they consider are who to post their details on the web, why they are looking at particular ads, or whether to download particular big files. These are all questions faced daily by individuals with digital literacy. Others will inevitably be making decisions about consent to perform other tasks, such as switching on the TV or Hoover. However, the questions are unchanged: "What will happen to the information that I provide?" and "Why do I need to provide the data for that to occur?" So, for a DC model to be valuable across populations, something needs to be looked at in some detail, namely recording at which point consent decision-making needs to be made and, in terms of what, of the vast amounts of data generated are retained and stored.

This broader debate of the digital divide must be considered, including utilizing online services without knowledge of the implications of sharing data, the firms one is dealing with, and the risks and data accumulation incurred. This then creates broader societal issues. One is whether research subjects and patients want to take the responsibility and control provided by the interactive dynamics of a DC approach or prefer to leave that to others. The question is who should control their data, how it should be handled, and who should be responsible.

In addition, for the DC strategy to be effective, people must be able to master their participation, be capable, willing, and able to act, and have access to correct representations of what is happening in their online interactions (Pendse et al., 2024). DC enthusiasts already understand how difficult it is to make these platforms participatory rather than performative for data sharers. However, there is hope that participation from the consumer technology industry will be immediate. Current efforts in DC platforms to generate consensual datasets are promising but do not put the control of the data in the hands of users.

2.4 Enhancing Organizational Efficiency

It is also broadly accepted that significant efficiency differences exist between health providers and that much is to be gained from the study and dissemination of best practices. Indeed, relative efficiency can be quantified by borrowing techniques from economics—such as data envelopment analysis and stochastic frontier analysis—to compare decision-making units with similar activities. Valuable lessons were derived and learned from the analytical tool, for example, the conducive to identifying the areas from which inefficient units could draw lessons from their more efficient counterparts and pinpointing which organizational factors contribute to higher levels of efficiency. The ultimate objective of structured data analysis and digital media use is to provide healthcare and medical organizations with the proper insight, clear-cut data, and analysis (as well as corrector) tools for optimizing and allocating resources to improve overall efficiency and effectiveness (Jahanbakhsh & Amini, 2023).

So, those tools will contribute toward an extra sustainable and patient-targeted healthcare gadget to gain people, communities, and society in the long run. This information-driven healthcare paradigm shift is sweepingly converting fitness care in many ways. One of the greater potentials of using data and information technology is enabling operational efficiency and optimal allocation of resources within a healthcare organization. Going deeper into the complex world of healthcare organizations will help us understand exactly how data is being harnessed to revolutionize healthcare. Characteristically, healthcare agencies have trailed in the back of completely exploiting data generation. Insufficient resources and funding have been dedicated to IT, with two running prices channeled into this critical area. This is minimal compared to different industries that spend approximately 6% to 8% of their operating costs on IT. However, there has been a dramatic change in recent years as healthcare groups are now spending more on IT, and there has also been a cultural shift in terms of the digitization of key information and rapid conversion to electronic health records (Keith et al., 2024). The dramatic change occurring now is, first and foremost, a response to the pressure to cut costs, along with an acute realization that proper information management can affect patient outcomes in a significant way. The new economic stimulus package hastened this shift, passed by the United States, and opened the doors to an even higher spending increase on IT. All kinds of innovative technologies are being accepted enthusiastically by healthcare organizations to obtain associated incentives and to take their operations to new heights of excellence. The healthcare industry is very complex and, at the same time, multifaceted; it requires innovation and adaptation to meet the ever-changing needs of both patients and providers. Concerning rising costs and demands to raise the quality of care in healthcare organizations battling an aging population, data-driven solutions and advanced analytics are among the most promising strategies.

Analytics holds immense power in gaining valuable insights from large amounts of information that enable organizations to make informed decisions, optimize resource allocation, improve patient outcomes, and smoothen operations. Healthcare organizations use several other means to better use data in this context. One of those techniques relates to imposing digital fitness information, revolutionizing the gathering, storage, and sharing of healthcare information. EHRs facilitate clean coordination and verbal exchange among most distinct healthcare companies to ensure access to suitable and well-timed statistics along the continuum of care (Dhote et al., 2024). This complements performance and effectiveness in healthcare transport, promotes affected person safety, and reduces healthcare prices. Another factor pertains to predictive analytics in picking out styles and trends in affected person facts for proactive interventions and personalized care. Healthcare corporations can expect ailment courses by analyzing patient information records and applying machine learning algorithms to their development prediction. This no longer advances the fitness consequences for personal patients; however, it additionally holds a place in population fitness control and the overall sustainability of the healthcare system. Also, with state-of-the-art technology like artificial intelligence and gadgets gaining knowledge, healthcare groups are growing their investment in absolutely knowing their fact's ability. AI and ML algorithms interpret complex medical statistics by revealing hidden styles and help fitness carriers diagnose and treat sicknesses. These technologies can change drug discovery, medical research, and patient-centered precision medicine strategy planning. There are challenges that healthcare practitioners have to overcome to benefit from these opportunities for collaboration with data.

The issues of data privacy and security are at large, more so because they involve sensitive health information. Strong safeguards with encryption measures must be implemented to ensure patient confidentiality, probably in compliance with the set regulations. Interoperability issues are significant hindrances to the free flow of data across varied health systems and providers. Standards, norms, and data-sharing paradigms are being proposed to bridge such barriers and ensure the free flow of information (Dhote et al., 2024). Today's healthcare organizations are realizing the tremendous potential of data to provide enhanced operating efficiency, enhanced patient outcomes, and assisted innovation.

That is, investment into IT will grow, and the digitization of healthcare information will change the industry remarkably. Only through the power of data analytics, predictive modeling, and advanced technologies can healthcare organizations begin to pave the way for a future of data-driven decision-making and individualized care. Against the backdrop of constantly evolving change in this sector, it behooves healthcare organizations to take up these changes in a manner that keeps them at the forefront of technological advancement while continuing to deliver high-quality, patient-centered care (Keith et al., 2024). They will contribute to a more sustainable, patient-centered healthcare system, reaping rewards for people, communities, and society. Moreover, information analytics identifies styles and traits in patient records and helps proactive intervention and personalization. By analyzing historical cases and using machine learning algorithms, disease development will be predictable, bad events will be avoided, and any healthcare organization will optimize its treatment plans positively. This advances individual patient outcomes and has potential applications for population health management and sustainability in the healthcare system. Besides this, health organizations are falling back on AI and ML to access data power. AI- and ML-based algorithms can access complex science data, identify concealed patterns, and help fitness professionals determine the correct diagnosis and treatment. Moreover, they can revolutionize scientific research and drug discovery and broaden precision medicinal drug methods tailor-made for unique sufferers. However, to apply the maximum electricity of facts, healthcare corporations will want to triumph over the subsequent challenges. Data privacy and security must become a very high priority, as is the sensitivity of healthcare information to a person. Encryption must be implemented to guarantee patient confidentiality and, on the other hand, the possibility of using large-scale healthcare data for the greater good in science and development and effective data exchange and collaboration among healthcare systems and providers (Holmes et al., 2023). Efforts are underway toward organizing standardized protocols and fact-sharing frameworks to surmount such barriers to the free flow of facts. This will ensure that fitness establishments can understand big skills in records to improve operational efficiency and decorate fitness effects and innovations. The accelerated funding in IT and the digitization of healthcare data are poised to revolutionize the sector dramatically. Only through advanced technology powered by information analytics and predictive modeling can healthcare agencies truly pave the way to a destiny where statistics-pushed choice-making and customized care may be a trendy component of healthcare delivery. As the world keeps converting, it becomes essential for healthcare businesses to embody and adapt to change if they live at the vanguard of technological advancement and supply nice, patient-focused care. This will assist in developing a greater sustainable, patient-targeted healthcare device, reaping benefits to the person, community, and society. One need not underestimate the options for data-driven care as limitless; hence, by embracing the paradigm shift, healthcare organizations can transform the industry and change healthcare delivery for good (Holmes et al., 2023). On this count, healthcare organizations examine various options that offer the best use of data. One system is warehousing, storing, and conveying healthcare data, which comprises an extensive electronic health record adoption system. EHRs facilitate coordination and effective communication among and between providers to provide current and accurate information throughout the continuum of care. To a large degree, this is achieved in enhanced healthcare effectiveness and efficiency, patient safety, and healthcare cost savings. Another area of focus is predictive analytics, which establishes trends and patterns in patient data to enable anticipatory intervention and patient-centered care. In addition, newer technologies like machine learning and artificial intelligence are being adopted by hospitals into their framework as a means of harnessing all the possible data has to offer. These algorithms and AI tools sift through complex healthcare data, identify embedded patterns, and allow healthcare professionals to develop a proper diagnoses for treatment. Healthcare organizations can apply machine learning algorithms to analyze patients' historical data for disease progression prediction, avoiding adverse events, and creating optimal treatment plans. This will help the individual patients and contribute to population health management and the general sustainability of healthcare. Data can achieve paradigm-shifting advances in functional performance, patient quality, and innovation and is already being emerging in healthcare organizations at a frenzied rate. With increasing investments in information technology and electronic care, the industry is only at the threshold of an unprecedented phenomenon. These technologies hold immense possibilities for changing the future of medical research, drug discovery, and the development of precision medicine approaches tailored for patients. Achieving effective data use will require several health organizations to overcome challenges that hinder fluent data exchange and coordinated efforts across health systems and providers (Keith et al., 2024). Some activities are currently underway to find solutions for these challenges through the execution of standardized protocols and frames for sharing data. Healthcare organizations are only beginning to realize the huge potential of data in enhancing operational efficiency, improving patient outcomes, and driving innovation. How the industry works is expected to change dramatically with an increased investment in information technology and digitization of health information. Equipped with the power of data analytics, predictive modeling, and advanced technologies, a healthcare organization can chart a course toward a future where data-driven decision-making and personalized care would be the standard (Holmes et al., 2023). In a continuously changing sector, healthcare organizations need to internalize these changes and live up to them to remain at the leading edge of technological progress and ensure the delivery of quality patient-centered care. By so doing, they will help develop a more sustainable and patient-centered healthcare system to benefit people, communities, and society. Also, organizational designs have their part to play in the sense that adopting digital health innovations can be encouraged. Dynamic and interactive designs to make more informed decisions and engage more can be a game-changer. Healthcare organizations will chart the way forward to a future characterized by data-driven decision-making and precision care through data analytics, predictive modeling, and advanced technologies. As the sector transforms, it devolves upon the healthcare organization to embrace and adapt to these changes in such a way as to stay at the forefront of technological strides while providing quality care that remains patient-centered (Gurley et al., 2021).

Healthcare in this millennial epoch has undergone an immense paradigmatic shift from conventional practice to a technocratic one, mainly trying to squeeze out efficiency and save cost. Today's critical healthcare challenges are hidden in the system's vast data. Properly harnessed data can speak volumes about many systemic issues currently dogging the healthcare sector (Basulo-Ribeiro & Teixeira, 2024).

2.5 Innovations in Digital Healthcare Solutions

On the other hand, organizational aspects of innovations in digital healthcare form the basis for the successful implementation and furtherance of healthcare technologies. Simultaneously, the rapid evolution of digital health solutions has changed the character of organizations' operations, imposing efficient management strategies and necessary adjustments to these innovations.

One of the organizational attributes incorporates strong leadership and communication in healthcare institutions. Since new technologies are invented, it is then upon the leaders of healthcare institutions to foster and create a culture that supports and promotes digital healthcare solutions (Fagherazzi et al., 2020). It will set the objectives of an organization in supporting these technologies, and stakeholders shall be enlightened about the benefits and challenges of the technologies (Journeault et al., 2021).

Organizational structures are instrumental in supporting the implementation of digital healthcare innovations. In this respect, flexible and agile structures that speed up decision-making and collaboration can be vital (Hermes et al., 2020; Sheikh et al., 2021). Therefore, cross-functional teams comprising professionals from a range of disciplines—for instance, clinicians, IT specialists, data scientists, and administrators—can guarantee comprehensive and holistic ways of approaching the implementation of digital healthcare solutions from a general perspective. Another critical aspect is effective change management. Preparing the workforce for new technologies through training programs, workshops, and constant continuous support is necessary for workers to remain innovative and build up digital competencies—a culture for which learning and improvement will be critical. Finally, partnerships and collaborations conducted in digital health concern external players. These include technology vendors, regulatory bodies, research institutions, and other healthcare providers sharing knowledge, good practices, and resources. This kind of collaboration enables innovations to be integrated into current healthcare systems and, therefore, are scalable and sustainable. Moreover, organizational aspects consider data privacy, security, and governance. Any digital solution in health means collecting, storing, and analyzing sensitive data about patients' information; hence, robust frameworks must be in place first to protect data privacy and, therefore, patients' trust. Organizational aspects are critical to implementing innovations in digital healthcare. Specifically, strong leadership, clear communications, flexible structures, strategies for change management, collaborations, and data governance set the critical elements that would drive this advancement in this fast-developing area. This is so because, with these aspects in place, a healthcare organization would be better positioned to tap into the power of digital technologies to drive better patient outcomes and healthcare service delivery transformation.

Developments in Telemedicine Technology: Digital health innovations within the boundaries of healthcare mean new digital technological tools and services that the digital health industry can offer. All of them are grounded in integrating the digital world with biomedical and genetic data, information technology, telecommunication, and personal medical devices. Singh et al., 2021; Haleem et al., 2022. This paradigm shift shall ride on the upcoming perceptions and data processing algorithms, inferring predictions based on simple flowchart logic with sufficient data inputs from biological sensors. Fully encrypted, hacking-proof data exchanges shall be routine—something utterly alien to the current practice.

The stakeholders can deliberate the laid-down procedures using empirical evidence to create an action program. All these innovations and developments are changing the face of healthcare. Telemedicine is an area challenging the boundaries of medical and clinical practice. The pace of growth can be seen in videoconferencing, Internet, telecommunications, wireless data, direct digital imaging and reporting, digital product databases, etc. (Zhou et al., 2023)—digital cameras, mobile phones, remote monitoring tools, etc. Since telemedicine is part of digital healthcare, the latter is broader and more sensitive. Telemedicine intervention, which comes with a convenience factor, is revolutionizing disease management and the delivery of clinical services. It gives patients and health professionals more leverage in accessing information and expertise. According to Mbunge et al. (2022), DHC is currently the generic term for telemedicine and related health information technology. There is a difference, and each has relative peripheral implications that must be understood accordingly (Bredenberg, 2023).

With a large-scale growth in healthcare data, AI and Machine Learning tools have come to the forefront of all technological innovations in healthcare, powering a revolution in treatment decision-making, care planning, patient outcomes, and resource alignment. In such a vast field as medicine, AI and machine learning tools can comb through colossal data sets and pull up the most pertinent information, ensuring that each diagnosis or medical advice meted out is accurate and complete with insight. This has been such a successful approach that the global machine-learning healthcare market was worth $11.9 billion as of early 2022 (Lipizzi, 2024).

AI is a generic term describing technologies that endow computing systems with human-like intelligence, such as understanding natural language or self-driven decision-making. It could be spotting the critical features of a phenomenon or having the ability to make decisions based on similar past experiences. AI-driven healthcare solutions disrupt various areas, from diagnostics and treatment planning to vision and object recognition, and finally to patient-oriented family caregiving. Diagnostics and treatment scenarios increasingly apply AI and machine learning in several cases. AI—led by neural networks—has proven performance at least as good as, or even superior to, human experts in multiple diagnostic fields, such as radiological imaging, pathology, or dermatological findings. AI can pick up on minute clinical features within enormous image datasets that were probably overlooked by tired or overwhelmed human examiners, with detection accuracies—on chest X-ray TB, for instance—surpassing those of human ones. AI can use this vast bank of accumulated data to develop real-time forecasting tools and generate reliable individual risk assessments.

Wearable technology has found its way into everyday life for thousands, if not millions. From smart glasses to fitness clothing, everything is fit with sensors to monitor some aspect of our health or daily habits, including digital jewelry like smartwatches. These technologies become even more powerful when combined with remote monitoring. They can also uniquely contribute to the patient's overall health and daily activities or changes in activity. For several years now, smaller monitoring devices have been available that can contact emergency services in the event of a catastrophic event in health, like a fall or heart attack. With the advancement in technology, these devices could improve overall health. Therefore, it allows its users to be more responsible for their health and wellness (Philip et al., 2021).

Suppose we want to appreciate and understand the real power behind watching these developments. In that case, we must focus on the advanced systems that allow these devices to work. From devices like Fitbit, which tracks everything from sleep to exercise including heart rate, to devices like Oura—a ring-like device designed only for tracking sleep—these are just a couple out of many varieties that will change remote patient monitoring as we know it today. The ability of these wearable devices to encourage patient compliance and act as a continuous aid to transformation across the patient's health makes them just a few ways in which health systems can leverage this kind of innovative integration to improve the quality of care. Wearable technologies represent just a tiny sliver of the digital forces aligning to redefine, upgrade, or otherwise re-shift the way we view healthcare moving into the future (Sargsyan, 2024).

This offers enormous potential for digital healthcare applications to improve patient care while reducing costs. However, significant challenges to using digital healthcare applications should be addressed. The first of these is privacy. Getting patients on board and willing to use these systems in the first place is essential, and consent to share their data with others is critical. While the public claims to favor this, there is a deep-seated objection to sharing their data (Keshta & Odeh, 2021).

A further problem is the fragmentation of systems and the integration of health data from many sources. There are concerns about interoperability issues and ownership of the health data from the various devices and services. This is where blockchain technology can make these systems more transparent, accessible, and secure. Evidence of this promise lies in the growing interest and investments from financial and start-up companies in developing digital healthcare systems through blockchain technology (Thapa & Camtepe, 2021).

Trends in using graph databases in making predictions by looking at various associations between people with similar diseases/health conditions and predicting the type of disease they will get or what treatments they will respond to (Senbekov et al., 2020). There is plenty of potential investment in data protection, but much work needs to be done.

The digital healthcare systems that provide predictive, preventive, personalized, and participatory healthcare, otherwise called "PH" health, are equally important. While many companies claim to do so, actual capabilities still need to be improved. PHealth is the leading edge of the following digital healthcare revolution (Wang et al., 2021).

References

Ahmed, S. (2019). BYOD, Personal Area Networks (PANs) and IOT: Threats to patients privacy.

Alzghaibi H. (2023). An examination of large-scale electronic health records implementation in Primary Healthcare Centers in Saudi Arabia: a qualitative study.

Awad, A., Trenfield, S. J., Pollard, T. D., Ong, J. J., Elbadawi, M., McCoubrey, L. E., Goyanes, A., Gaisford, S., & Basit, A. W. (2021). Connected healthcare: Improving patient care using digital health technologies. *Advanced Drug Delivery Reviews, 178*, 113958. https://doi.org/10.1016/j.addr.2021.113958. Epub 2021 Sep 1. PMID: 34478781.

Barbazzeni, B., Haider, S., Friebe, M. (2022). Engaging through awareness: Purpose-driven framework development to evaluate and develop future business strategies with exponential technologies toward healthcare democratization.

Barrett, M., & Orlikowski, W. (2021). Scale matters: Doing practice-based studies of contemporary digital phenomena. *MIS Quarterly, 45*(1), 467–472.

Basulo-Ribeiro, J., & Teixeira, L. (2024). The future of healthcare with industry 5.0: preliminary interview-based qualitative analysis. *Future Internet, 16*(3), 68.

Bredenberg, E. (2023). Digital care pathway for type 2 diabetes patients–The experiences and opinions of diabetes specialist nurses.

Budd, J., Miller, B. S., Manning, E. M. et al. (2020). Digital technologies in the public-health response to COVID-19. *Nature Medicine, 26*, 1183–1192. https://doi.org/10.1038/s41591-020-1011-4

Chandra, A., Martin, L. T., Acosta, J. D., Nelson, C., Yeung, D., Qureshi, N., & Blagg, T. (2022). Equity as a guiding principle for the public health data system. *Big Data, 10*(S1), S3–S8.

Cordeiro, J. V. (2021). Digital technologies and data science as health enablers: An outline of appealing promises and compelling ethical, legal, and social challenges. *Frontiers in Medicine*.

Crispo, B., Roveri, M., Pinto, S., Gomes, T., Pasic, A., Milankovich, A., Puron, D., Garcia, A., Putrle, Z., Ten, P., & Catalano, M. (2024). CROSSCON: Cross-platform open security stack for connected devices. *arXiv preprint arXiv:2406.03401*.

Dang, J., King, K. M., & Inzlicht, M. (2020). Why Are Self-Report and Behavioral Measures Weakly Correlated? *Trends in Cognitive Sciences, 24*(4), 267–269. https://doi.org/10.1016/j.tics.2020.01.007. Epub 2020 Feb 17. PMID: 32160564; PMCID: PMC7977810.

Dhote, S., Deogaonkar, A., & Vichoray, C. (2024, March). Striving for Balance: Women Entrepreneurs in India, and Their Multiple Gendered Roles During COVID-19. In 2024 IEEE International Conference on Interdisciplinary Approaches in Technology and Management for Social Innovation (IATMSI) (Vol. 2, pp. 1-6). IEEE.

Fagherazzi, G., Goetzinger, C., Rashid, M. A., Aguayo, G. A., & Huiart, L. (2020). Digital health strategies to fight COVID-19 worldwide: Challenges, recommendations, and a call for papers. *Journal of Medical Internet Research, 22*(6), e19284.

Goffman, T. E., & Glatstein, E. (2004). The vulnerability of radiation oncology within the medical-industrial complex. *International Journal of Radiation Oncology Biology Physics*. https://doi.org/10.1016/j.ijrobp.2003.12.026

Golinelli, D., Boetto, E., Carullo, G., Nuzzolese, A. G., Landini, M. P., & Fantini, M. P. (2020). Adoption of Digital Technologies in Health Care During the COVID-19 Pandemic: Systematic Review of Early Scientific Literature. *Journal of Medical Internet Research, 22*(11), e22280. https://doi.org/10.2196/22280. PMID: 33079693; PMCID: PMC7652596.

Gurley, L., Roberson, J., York, A. B., & Childress, J. (2021). Interprofessional team approach using standardized patient simulation to facilitate person-centered quality healthcare in home hospice care setting. *Journal of Hospice & Palliative Nursing, 23*(1), 69–77.

Haleem, A., Javaid, M., Singh, R. P., & Suman, R. (2022). Medical 4.0 technologies for health-care: Features, capabilities, and applications. *Internet of Things and Cyber-Physical Systems, 2*, 12–30.

Hamid, Z., Khalique, F., Mahmood, S., Daud, A., Bukhari, A., & Alshemaimri, B. (2024). Healthcare insurance fraud detection using data mining. *BMC Medical Informatics and Decision Making., 24*(1), 112.

Hermes, S., Riasanow, T., Clemons, E. K., Böhm, M., & Krcmar, H. (2020). The digital transformation of the healthcare industry: Exploring the rise of emerging platform ecosystems and their influence on the role of patients. *Business Research, 13*(3), 1033–1069.

Holmes, J., Liu, Z., Zhang, L., Ding, Y., Sio, T. T., McGee, L. A., ... & Liu, W. (2023). Evaluating large language models on a highly-specialized topic, radiation oncology physics. *Frontiers in Oncology, 13*, 1219326.

Hourani, D, Darling, S, Cameron, E, Dromey, J et al. (2021). What makes for a successful digital health integrated program of work? Lessons learnt and recommendations from the Melbourne Children's Campus.

Jahanbakhsh Javid, N., & Amini, M. (2023). Evaluating the effect of supply chain management practice on implementation of halal agroindustry and competitive advantage for small and medium enterprises. *International Journal of Computer Science and Information Technology, 15*(2023), 8997–9008.

Janarthanan, V., Nagrale, N. V., Singh, O. G., Raj, K. V., & Singh, G. (2024). Legal and ethical issues associated with challenges in the implementation of the electronic medical record system and its current laws in India. *Cureus, 16*(3).

Journeault, M., Perron, A., & Vallières, L. (2021). The collaborative roles of stakeholders in supporting the adoption of sustainability in SMEs. *Journal of Environmental Management.*

Keith, G. A., Woodward, R. A., Hopkins, T., Allwood-Spiers, S., Trinder, J., Muir, K. W., ... & Fullerton, N. E. (2024). Towards clinical translation of 7 Tesla MRI in the human brain. *IPEM-Translation, 9*, 100025.

Keshta, I., & Odeh, A. (2021). Security and privacy of electronic health records: Concerns and challenges. *Egyptian Informatics Journal.*

Krishnamoorthy, S., Dua, A. & Gupta, S. (2023). Role of emerging technologies in future IoT-driven Healthcare 4.0 technologies: a survey, current challenges and future directions. *Journal of Ambient Intelligence and Humanized Computing, 14*, 361–407. https://doi.org/10.1007/s12652-021-03302-w

Kulikowski, C. A. (2022). Ethics in the history of medical informatics for decision-making: Early challenges to digital health goals.

Landesz, T., Varghese, S., & Sargsyan, K. (Eds.). (2023). *Future intelligence: The world in 2050 - Enabling governments, innovators, and businesses to create a better future*. Springer.

Lin, J. C., Gillette, J. S., Zhu, A. S., French, D. D., Weir, M., Meyers, D. J., & Greenberg, P. B. (2025). Outcomes of price transparency policies for healthcare services in the United States: A systematic review. *Health Policy and Technology*, 100973.

Lipizzi, C. (2024). Societal impacts of artificial intelligence and machine learning.

Maleka, N. H., & Matli, W. (2024). A review of telehealth during the COVID-19 emergency situation in the public health sector: Challenges and opportunities. *Journal of Science and Technology Policy Management, 15*(4), 707–724.

Manias, E., Kusljic, S., & Wu, A. (2020). Interventions to reduce medication errors in adult medical and surgical settings: a systematic review. *Therapeutic Advances in Drug Safety, 12*(11), 2042098620968309. https://doi.org/10.1177/2042098620968309. PMID: 33240478; PMCID: PMC7672746.

Marques, I. C., & Ferreira, J. J. (2020). Digital transformation in the area of health: systematic review of 45 years of evolution. *Health and Technology, 10*(3), 575–586.

Massaro, M. (2023). Digital transformation in the healthcare sector through blockchain technology. Insights from academic research and business developments, *Technovation, 120*, 102386, ISSN 0166-4972. https://doi.org/10.1016/j.technovation.2021.102386.

Mbunge, E., Muchemwa, B., & Batani, J. (2021). Sensors and healthcare 5.0: Transformative shift in virtual care through emerging digital health technologies. *Global Health Journal.*

Mbunge, E., Muchemwa, B., & Batani, J. (2022). *Are we there yet? Unbundling the potential adoption and integration of telemedicine to improve virtual healthcare services in African health systems*. Sensors International.

Miller, A. S., & Payne, B. R. (2016). Health IT security: An examination of modern challenges in maintaining HIPAA and HITECH compliance.

Naib, P., Gupta, S. D., & Chandrashekar, S. (2024). Study of provider perceptions of types and extent of fraud in health insurance and factors influencing ethics in healthcare provisioning: Learnings from world's largest public health insurance scheme in India. *Journal of Health Management, 27*, 09720634241304983.

Nijor, S., Rallis, G., Lad, N., & Gokcen, E. (2022). Patient Safety Issues From Information Overload in Electronic Medical Records. *Journal of Patient Safety, 18*(6), e999-e1003. https://doi.org/10.1097/PTS.0000000000001002. Epub 2022 Apr 7. PMID: 35985047; PMCID: PMC9422765.

Nebeker, C., Torous, J., Bartlett Ellis, R. J. (2019). Building the case for actionable ethics in digital health research supported by artificial intelligence.

Pendse, S. R., Stapleton, L., Kumar, N., De Choudhury, M., et al. (2024). Advancing a consent-forward paradigm for digital mental health data.

Philip, N. Y., Rodrigues, J. J., Wang, H., Fong, S. J., & Chen, J. (2021). Internet of Things for in-home health monitoring systems: Current advances, challenges and future directions. *IEEE Journal on Selected Areas in Communications, 39*(2), 300–310.

Pulimamidi, R. (2024). To enhance customer (or patient) experience based on IoT analytical study through technology (IT) transformation for E-healthcare. *Measurement: Sensors.*

Sargsyan, K. (2024). Artificial Intelligence and Machine Learning: Technologies revolutionizing the healthcare sector and biomedical research. *Innovations in Digital Health, Diagnostics, and Biomarkers, 4*, 50–52. https://doi.org/10.36401/IDDB-24-X2

Senbekov, M., Saliev, T., Bukeyeva, Z., Almabayeva, A., Zhanaliyeva, M., Aitenova, N., Toishibekov, Y., & Fakhradiyev, I. (2020). The recent progress and applications of digital technologies in healthcare: A review. *International Journal of Telemedicine and Applications, 2020*(1), 8830200.

Sharma, M., & Joshi, S. (2021). Barriers to blockchain adoption in healthcare industry: An Indian perspective. *Journal of Global Operations and Strategic Sourcing, 14*(1), 134–169.

Sheikh, A., Anderson, M., Albala, S., Casadei, B., Franklin, B. D., Richards, M., Taylor, D., Tibble, H., & Mossialos, E. (2021). Health information technology and digital innovation for national learning health and care systems. *The Lancet Digital Health, 3*(6), e383–e396.

Singh, S., Bhatt, P., Sharma, S. K., & Rabiu, S. (2021). Digital transformation in healthcare: Innovation and technologies. In *Blockchain for healthcare systems* (pp. 61–79). CRC Press.

Sipanoun, P., Oulton, K., Gibson, K., & Wray, J. (2022). The experiences and perceptions of users of an electronic patient record system in a pediatric hospital setting: a systematic review. *International Journal of Medical Informatics, 160.* https://doi.org/10.1016/j.ijmedinf.2022.104691

Spinean, A., Carniciu, S., Mladin, O. A., & Serafinceanu, C. (2024). The transformative power of mHealth apps: empowering patients with obesity and diabetes–a narrative review. *Journal of Medicine and Life, 17*(12), 1030.

Stefanicka-Wojtas, D., & Kurpas, D. (2022). eHealth and mHealth in chronic diseases—Identification of barriers, existing solutions, and promoters based on a survey of EU stakeholders involved in Regions4PerMed (H2020).

Teare, H. J. A., Prictor, M., & Kaye, J. (2020). Reflections on dynamic consent in biomedical research: the story so far.

Thapa, C., & Camtepe, S. (2021). Precision health data: Requirements, challenges and existing techniques for data security and privacy. *Computers in Biology and Medicine.*

Trout, K. E., Chen, L. W., Wilson, F. A., Tak, H. J., & Palm, D. (2022). The Impact of Meaningful Use and Electronic Health Records on Hospital Patient Safety. *The International Journal of Environmental Research and Public Health, 19*(19), 12525. https://doi.org/10.3390/ijerph191912525. PMID: 36231824; PMCID: PMC9564815.

Wang, Q., Su, M., Zhang, M., & Li, R. (2021). Integrating digital technologies and public health to fight Covid-19 pandemic: Key technologies, applications, challenges and outlook of digital healthcare. *International Journal of Environmental Research and Public Health, 18*(11), 6053.

Wu, J., Qiao, J., Nicholas, S., Liu, Y., & Maitland, E. (2022). The challenge of healthcare big data to China's commercial health insurance industry: Evaluation and recommendations. *BMC Health Services Research., 22*(1), 1189.

Yao, R., Zhang, W., Evans, R., Cao, G., Rui, T., & Shen, L. (2022). Inequities in health care services caused by the adoption of digital health technologies: scoping review. *Journal of Medical Internet Research, 24*(3), e34144.

Zhou, M., Li, X., & Burtch, G. (2023). *Healthcare across boundaries: Urban-rural differences in the consequences of telehealth adoption.* Information Systems Research.

Organization of People and Behavioral Insights

3

Angeliki Koltsida, Io Hong Cheong, and Zisis Kozlakidis

The organization of people is equivalent to understanding people's behavior, which is particularly important in healthcare. The organization of people involves recognizing the diverse factors and interactions that influence how professionals understand and provide care and how individuals seek, receive, and adhere to medical advice and treatments. These behaviors are shaped by medical facts and a complex interplay of psychological, social, cultural, and economic factors. For example, psychological aspects include personal beliefs, health literacy (including digital literacy), and past experiences with healthcare systems. Social influences encompass family, community, and societal norms, while cultural elements involve traditional practices and values around health and wellness. Economic considerations, such as remuneration levels, access to care (including universal health coverage), insurance coverage, and the affordability of treatments, also play a critical role.

Several studies have been published on the above aspects, describing these factors allows healthcare providers to better address barriers to effective care and improve patient engagement, ultimately leading to better health outcomes. This chapter will focus on the organization of people, particularly professionals, for delivering patient-centered care, improving health outcomes, and optimizing healthcare delivery. We will illustrate how insights from practical experiences and evidence-based practices catalyze positive change within health systems by looking at Leadership, the teams, and the activities required to support the dynamics of healthcare excellence.

A. Koltsida · I. H. Cheong · Z. Kozlakidis (✉)
Laboratory Services and Biobanking, International Agency for Research on Cancer, World Health Organization, Lyon, France
e-mail: kozlakidisz@iarc.who.int

B. Alknawy (ed.), *Organizational Insights: Healthcare Perspective*, Springer Series in Healthcare Management and Innovation,
https://doi.org/10.1007/978-3-032-10532-5_3

3.1 Leadership Styles and Healthcare

> Good l/eaders provide two things: clear, consistent direction, and the desire in other people to follow the direction set. One out of two does not make a good leader
>
> Ben Gowland, What is the role of Leadership in the NHS? (2016)

Leadership is paramount in healthcare, as it is a field of activity determined by hierarchies and often rigid performance frameworks. Effective Leadership frequently involves a combination of different styles tailored to the organization's needs, the team's characteristics, and the challenges of the healthcare environment. Leaders may adapt their leadership style based on the situation, leveraging their strengths and capabilities to inspire, motivate, and empower their teams to achieve excellence in patient care and organizational performance. From a behavioral perspective, various leadership styles have been employed within different contexts to effectively manage teams, inspire innovation, and drive organizational success. These styles are often categorized as (Perez, 2021):

Transformational Leadership involves inspiring and motivating teams through a compelling vision, fostering innovation, and empowering individuals to reach their potential (Bass & Riggio, 2006). These leaders lead by example, encourage collaboration, and cultivate a culture of continuous growth. This style is especially effective in driving organizational change and achieving long-term strategic goals in healthcare. For instance, in countries like Vietnam, Malaysia, and Australia, pharmaceutical industries aligned infrastructure with organizational structure, production, and national needs. The pandemic accelerated this, with Australia establishing large-scale mRNA vaccine manufacturing—operational at Monash University by 2024 (The Premier of Victoria, 2023).

A distinctly different style is Servant Leadership, where servant leaders prioritize the needs of others and focus on serving the interests of their team members, patients, and communities. They emphasize empathy, compassion, and humility and actively seek to support and develop their team members (Perez, 2021). Servant leaders empower individuals to take ownership of their work, foster a culture of trust and collaboration, and prioritize patient-centered care in healthcare organizations. Servant Leadership is often considered to be fitting the healthcare mission (McCann et al., 2014). However, this approach may not always be culturally acceptable and cannot deal with all of the current healthcare complexity challenges, particularly where goal-driven decisions require large-scale changes.

Transactional Leaders emphasize clear roles, expectations, and performance targets, focusing on rewards and incentives in exchange for results. This approach highlights accountability, efficiency, and adherence to established protocols, making it well-suited for managing routine operations and ensuring regulatory compliance in healthcare settings (Richards, 2020). While effective for day-to-day tasks, it may not foster creativity or long-term engagement. For instance, transactional leadership assumes stakeholders are primarily reward-driven—yet in healthcare, motivation often stems from deeper emotional drivers.

Lastly, three leadership styles—authentic, democratic, and laissez-faire—are often discussed together, though they differ subtly. These can be seen as varying expressions of participative behavior, shaped by context. For example, democratic leadership, rooted in Western thought, may align with what other regions consider authentic leadership (Dorfman, 1996). These styles often overlap; a democratic leader involving staff in decisions may also be seen as authentic, fostering trust and shared accountability.

Authentic leaders are genuine, self-aware, and transparent, building trust and promoting shared decision-making in healthcare. Democratic leaders actively seek input and feedback, enhancing satisfaction through inclusive decisions. Laissez-faire leaders offer minimal guidance, allowing autonomy and independence—this can spark innovation but may also lead to ambiguity and reduced accountability, which can demotivate healthcare staff.

The critical role of Leadership can be demonstrated in a case study from the UK. Specifically, at Epsom and St Helier, an innovative process was introduced in 2018 for diagnosing patients with suspected prostate cancer and as an initial site for a national roll-out. This process was called the "Rapid (Rapid Assessment for Prostate Imaging and Diagnosis) prostate cancer pathway." It was part of the initial phase in the innovation diffusion that had been piloted in two teaching hospital locations previously (Eldred-Evans et al., 2023). Results from the earlier pilots in the teaching hospitals resulted in a 50% reduction in pathway time to diagnosis, reduced visits, and 43% fewer biopsies being required. Ensuring good clinical leadership and management support for the Rapid project from the outset was necessary, and this was demonstrated by different forms of leadership deployed by the same individuals in different contexts. Transformational Leadership supports knowledge sharing between clinical leaders working across organizations (Waring et al., 2013), specifically with regional South London clinical urology networks and the London cancer services sector. Clinical, nursing, and managerial groups are represented at that level, and leveraging their influence and recruiting their support was fundamental in pushing through the Rapid innovation pathway. Engaging with Prostate Cancer UK was a demonstration of servant Leadership, helping to frame a healthcare narrative whereby individual cases could be used to communicate a story around the benefits of the pathway at a patient level. This helped reinforce the benefits of innovation at the patient, clinician, and organizational levels.

Leaders can alter their communication style and information-sharing focus depending on what they understand about the audience—offering the appropriate insights tailored to the different audiences. This is important, as it helps align diverse groups towards a common goal. Additionally, other ways of viewing a problem are explored by redirecting the focus to areas they are more likely to engage with and reduce challenges with knowledge barriers. This is not possible through more passive forms of leadership, or even transactional leadership. Leaders should encourage people to shift from their standard self-protection stance (which has a low capacity to learn and improve) to reframe to a more explicit reflective/learning-orientated frame focused on a particular situation, as happened in Epsom and St Helier hospitals during the introduction of the Rapid pathway.

3.2 Team Dynamics and Interdisciplinary Collaboration

> We are what we repeatedly do. Excellence then, is not an act, but a habit.
> Aristotle as interpreted by Will Durant, The Story of Philosophy (1926).

A critical component of good Leadership is the shaping of the right team of individuals to serve the goals and initiatives the Leadership sets. As such, the leader is part of a team—in reality, of different overlapping teams—at any one time. The following parameters influence team dynamics and interdisciplinary collaboration in hospitals.

Leadership is vital in fostering teamwork, empowering staff, and creating supportive environments that promote collaboration and shared purpose in healthcare. This encourages transparency, accountability, and improved team cohesion. Effective leaders communicate openly, clearly, and timely, enabling information sharing, care coordination, and responsive patient care. Communication barriers—like language gaps, hierarchy, or poor channels—can hinder teamwork. Defining roles and responsibilities is essential, especially in interdisciplinary teams, to avoid ambiguity and clarify each member's scope and contribution.

Strong leadership communication helps establish shared goals aligned with patient needs and organizational priorities (Okpala, 2021). Clear goals provide direction, unify efforts, and support collaboration. For example, introducing new technologies requires implementation strategies tailored to both the innovation and the setting. This includes assessing knowledge transfer needs, team readiness, and necessary resources. Support should be adapted to the innovation and the culture and capacity of the stakeholders involved.

Beyond effective communication, mutual respect and trust are fundamental for building strong interpersonal relationships and fostering collaboration among teams of healthcare professionals. Respecting the expertise, perspectives, and contributions of colleagues from different disciplines promotes a culture of collaboration and encourages open dialogue and knowledge sharing. In healthcare, care is often provided through multidisciplinary teams. Introducing an aim or a change of practice, e.g., an innovation, requires assigning specific roles to specific individuals. In certain circumstances, additional patient support may be necessary to support a particular patient population served by the healthcare organization. Within the healthcare team, it will have to be agreed on how this additional requirement will be supported. For example, a team with a high number of nursing vacancies may assign roles to non-clinical and non-nursing staff whenever possible, an approach that might be different at another hospital with a shortage of experienced non-clinical staff.

It has been shown that supportive and transformational leadership styles are consistently associated with higher job satisfaction and lower turnover intentions among nurses, as they foster a sense of empowerment, recognition, and professional growth. This observation is consistent whether the study focuses on a single area, e.g., Ontario, Canada, (Boamah et al., 2018), or many different sites as part of a systematic review (Cummings et al., 2018). Conversely, poor leadership characterized by lack of support, unclear communication, and inadequate staffing can contribute to moral distress and emotional exhaustion, driving both nurses and physicians to leave their roles (Montgomery et al., 2019)—and when this becomes visible, it is already too late to address. Effective leadership can mitigate burnout by promoting a healthy work environment, encouraging teamwork, and ensuring manageable workloads (Shanafelt & Noseworthy, 2017). In particular, leaders who engage in open communication and shared decision-making help reduce feelings of isolation and depersonalization among physicians, key components of burnout (West et al., 2018).

Hospitals' organizational culture and structure can significantly influence team dynamics and interdisciplinary collaboration (Johnson et al., 2016). Cultures that value teamwork, innovation, and continuous learning promote collaboration and multidisciplinary care delivery. Supportive organizational structures, such as interdisciplinary care teams, collaborative practice models, and shared governance mechanisms, facilitate communication, coordination, and teamwork among healthcare professionals in hospitals. However, a supportive culture also needs to provide interprofessional education and training opportunities for healthcare professionals so that the culture becomes an integral part of the organization and can enhance the understanding of different roles, perspectives, and contributions within interdisciplinary teams. For instance, a 2024 randomized controlled trial conducted at Atatürk University in Turkey demonstrated that a structured interprofessional education program significantly improved medical and nursing students' attitudes, socialization, and valuing of interprofessional collaboration, underscoring the importance of integrating such training into healthcare curricula to foster effective teamwork and patient care from the very first step of a healthcare career (Tanrıverdi et al., 2025).

From an organizational perspective, interdisciplinary collaboration should be viewed as focusing on the potential to improve/complement rather than replace traditional care delivery methods, and ensuring it is understood as an iterative process that can be adapted and refined, so resistance to change can be reduced. From a clinician's perspective, highlighting the potential to address unmet needs or improve patient outcomes (i.e., as a solution to pressing challenges) can lead to support. It must align with the provider's priorities and values to feel relevant and accepted, ideally reducing rather than creating an administrative or time burden. From a support staff (non-clinical) angle, the process journey and administrative benefits are essential. To achieve this, a collaborative work environment is needed, one that values communication, Leadership, role clarity, mutual respect, shared goals, education, and supportive organizational culture. Hospitals that enhance team dynamics and interdisciplinary collaboration ultimately improve patient outcomes and healthcare delivery.

For example, the environmental sustainability agenda across healthcare facilities can only be driven by the team dynamics in the facility, requiring stakeholder engagement at a corporate level before locally focusing on how it is adopted on the frontline (for example, in the case of Cork University Hospital in Ireland (Ryan-Fogarty et al., 2016)). In considering the communications, some should be addressed to all staff, and some just to clinicians. For example, the all-staff emails can focus on framing environmental sustainability with a global, moral perspective: "This is the right thing for the planet," and action points are broken into things staff have control over, e.g., recycling and waste disposal actions, thinking before printing a document, not running the dishwasher until complete, etc. From a clinical perspective, the framing has to be more targeted to changing prescribing practices, e.g., swapping asthma inhaler prescriptions to ones without aerosols. From an organizational perspective, this can be supported by specific communications from the CEO, including promising % donations to a charity if targets are met in the next prescribing audit. This plays to the altruistic narrative embedded within healthcare. Finally, ringfenced, non-clinical staff time can be used to develop communication and implementation specificities beyond corporate support.

3.3 Talent Acquisition and Recruitment Strategies

As healthcare teams are assembled for specific tasks, so too are individual staff selected through a structured process. Effective workforce planning starts with forecasting future staffing needs based on patient demand and strategic goals, typically over a 3–5-year horizon. Hospitals identify skill gaps and create targeted recruitment strategies to attract talent aligned with their priorities. A strong employer brand—built on quality care, innovation, and supportive environments—is key to drawing qualified candidates. Competitive compensation, along with perks like tuition reimbursement, professional development, and work-life balance initiatives, further boosts appeal. Research highlights the importance of diversity and inclusion in recruitment to build culturally competent, multidisciplinary teams, supported by outreach, training, and inclusive practices (Khuntia et al., 2022). Investing in continuing education, leadership development, and AI training also enhances employee satisfaction and long-term retention. Current international literature supports that AI will augment rather than replace physicians. Frankly, it "cannot engage in high-level conversation or interaction with patients in order to gain their trust, reassure them, or express empathy, all of which are important parts of the doctor-patient relationship" (Akinrinmade et al., 2023). The human element in medicine cannot be replaced. Still, healthcare professionals must develop competency about artificial intelligence (AI) by formalizing it in the curricula of future physicians, leaving those who refuse to amass the essential skill sets behind without that competitive advantage. Indeed, "hybrid people"—with combined expertise—can be precious assets in innovation processes because they can speak confidently across different groups and build trust.

3.4 Employee Training and Development Programs: Engagement and Motivation

> The 2023 European Year of Skills was established to address skills shortages in the European Union … and boost the resilience in the healthcare sector.

European Union, Why a European Year of Skills? (2023)

Training and development programs provide insights into hospital staff's competencies, skills, and knowledge gaps. By assessing training needs and evaluating employee performance, hospitals can identify areas for improvement and tailor training initiatives to enhance the capabilities and effectiveness of their workforce. Research supports that employee training and development programs directly impact the quality of hospital patient care, as well-trained and skilled healthcare professionals are better equipped to provide safe, effective, patient-centered care. Training also provides two additional aspects: firstly, training and development programs play a crucial role in ensuring compliance with regulatory requirements, accreditation standards, and best practices in healthcare. Secondly, investing in employee training and development (e.g., leadership development) demonstrates a commitment by the healthcare organization to the professional growth and well-being of hospital staff. In turn, engaged and satisfied employees are more likely to deliver high-quality care, exhibit job satisfaction, and remain committed to their organizations, creating a succession pipeline.

Hospital employee training and development programs offer valuable insights into employee competencies, patient care quality, regulatory compliance, innovation, leadership development, and employee well-being. Micro-framing by key individuals who possess significant influence within their peer groups is pivotal for training to be seen as an opportunity rather than merely a requirement. According to Edmondson, "a frame is a set of assumptions and beliefs about a particular object or situation. The process of framing is a process of creating meaning." (Edmondson, 2003). "Frames affect both how we feel and how we think. Framing is neither bad nor good; it is inevitable, as we interpret what is happening around us through a lens shaped by our personal history and current social context." In healthcare, framing is crucial for the nuances of how information is presented or tailored to different stakeholder groups and the importance of emotional and cultural factors involved in processing and accepting the information received. For example, the training and development opportunities can be framed within an organization's overall organizational transformation effort, providing a sense of camaraderie and vested interest in attending—or simply can be framed as part of a transactional set of activities directly relevant to career progression. Either of those can be effective, depending on the culture and context of the organization. It has been almost half a century since the seminal study by Wilson et al., demonstrating the power of micro-framing in healthcare, where individuals were more willing to select riskier treatments when outcomes were presented accurately, yet in a positive rather than a negative context (Wilson et al., 1987). Since then, the study of framing information within healthcare has continued apace, and leveraging these insights can prove central to presenting and supporting training and development opportunities and fostering a culture of excellence in healthcare delivery.

Regarding staff engagement and motivation, the most impactful techniques in healthcare encompass recognition and appreciation programs, professional development and career advancement opportunities, employee feedback and involvement, and work-life balance initiatives. Implementing recognition and appreciation programs that acknowledge and celebrate employees' contributions is a powerful way to boost morale and motivation, with hospitals recognizing outstanding performance, teamwork, and patient care excellence through awards, commendations, and public acknowledgments. Regularly expressing appreciation for employees' efforts and achievements reinforces a culture of recognition and fosters a sense of pride and ownership among staff members, as shown in a study of a public health hospital in Cyprus (Lambrou et al., 2010) and other locations.

Providing opportunities for professional growth is key to engaging and motivating healthcare professionals. Investing in development boosts job satisfaction while driving organizational innovation and effectiveness. Encouraging staff involvement in decision-making fosters ownership and engagement. Hospitals worldwide use tools like surveys, suggestion boxes, and town hall meetings to gather employee feedback on care and operations. For instance, University Hospital Bristol NHS Foundation Trust in the UK introduced a real-time feedback app to capture staff experience and support leader-staff dialogue. Timely responses from managers to concerns proved essential, reinforcing trust and boosting job satisfaction. This responsiveness created a positive work environment and improved patient care. As a result, the app was sustained across both clinical and non-clinical departments (Frampton et al., 2017).

3.5 Performance Management and Appraisal Systems

> Appraisal is an effective way for individuals to identify their learning needs. In clinical governance, it is a means of enhancing quality in the NHS system.
>
> Maurice Conlon, director of GP appraiser training programme, UK (2003)

Effective leaders foster a culture of safety by promoting open communication, encouraging error reporting without fear of blame, and actively addressing systemic issues (Sammer et al., 2010). Transformational leadership, in particular, has been associated with reduced adverse events and higher perceptions of safety among staff (Wong et al., 2013). For example, a study conducted in Canadian hospitals found that units led by transformational leaders reported fewer medication errors and patient falls (Boamah et al., 2018). Leadership visibility and engagement—such as conducting safety WalkRounds—have also been shown to significantly improve frontline staff's confidence in safety protocols (Frankel et al., 2005). In the UK, implementation of structured leadership programs like the NHS Leadership Academy has contributed to measurable improvements in safety culture and incident response (West et al., 2014). Measuring these improvements and overall performance can take a number of different approaches.

At an individual level, performance in healthcare is measured through objective-based appraisals. Employees and their supervisors set specific, measurable, achievable, relevant, and time-bound (SMART) objectives or goals aligned with organizational priorities. Performance is evaluated based on the extent to which employees meet or exceed these objectives. Objective-based performance appraisal promotes clarity, accountability, and goal alignment, encouraging employees to focus on outcomes and results that contribute to organizational success. More holistic performance appraisal approaches exist, e.g., 360-degree feedback, involving gathering feedback from multiple sources, including supervisors, peers, subordinates, and sometimes external stakeholders such as patients or other healthcare professionals. While this feedback provides a comprehensive view of an employee's performance from various perspectives, it is time-costly and has been implemented in a fragmented fashion.

At a departmental unit or institution level, management by objectives (MBO) is a well-established performance management approach that emphasizes—in the ideal scenario—collaborative goal setting, planning, and performance evaluation between managers and employees. However, objectives are often directed in a top-down fashion, and performance is evaluated based on the achievement of these objectives. For example, many targets were set by the UK government for the NHS between 1996 and 2006 in an aggressive effort to manage the system's performance as a whole (Thorlby et al., 2019). While these targets were ambitious to push through reform and overall modernization opportunities, they have not been met consistently in the last decade (Thorlby et al., 2019) and have been blamed for distorting clinical priorities, as organizations need to consider achieving one target at the expense of another (Bevan & Hood, 2006). For example, ambulances have been forced to queue up outside busy emergency departments so that the hospital can meet its A&E target. In contrast, the ambulances might not be able to meet their target in responding to emergency calls (Alarilla et al., 2022).

Implementing the above is context-driven and also needs to consider the different levels of responsibility. For example, the concept of legal liability is important for clinicians, as generally, the onus has been on medical professionals to take responsibility for their advice as well as any use of medical devices in a clinical scenario, and the medical professional needs to fully understand the inputs and outputs for them to be responsible for the workings of the device (Saw & Ng, 2022).

3.6 Where Do Things Go Wrong?

Communication: When things go wrong in healthcare, organizational issues such as poor communication, inadequate staffing, and lack of resources often contribute to systemic failures, leading to compromised patient care and employee burnout. Behaviorally, a culture that discourages reporting mistakes, insufficient training and development of staff, and resistance to change can exacerbate problems, preventing timely interventions and continuous improvement. Let us consider a patient with depression who is prescribed antidepressants by their primary care physician. Suppose the physician does not take the time to explain the importance of medication adherence, potential side effects, and the expected timeline for seeing improvements. In that case, the patient might not understand how the medication works. Without this information, the patient might discontinue the medication prematurely if they do not feel immediate relief or if they experience side effects, believing the treatment is ineffective or harmful.

Additionally, if the physician does not communicate the availability of additional support, such as therapy or counselling services, the patient may not seek these complementary treatments. This suboptimal communication can result in suboptimal treatment outcomes and an increased risk of the patient's condition worsening. Often, frontline clinicians are delivered targets to meet and are faced with leadership-driven initiatives, such as cost savings. However, cost savings generally do not influence or sway frontline practitioners. Still, they can be helpful too if benefits to the service can be achieved and demonstrated, such as extra staff recruitment or administrative support.

Psychological biases: Taking the above into account, psychological biases, such as confirmation bias, can significantly impact medical decision-making, often leading to suboptimal patient care. Confirmation bias occurs when healthcare professionals favour information that supports their pre-existing beliefs or hypotheses, disregarding contradictory evidence. For example, a classic book by Nisbett and Ross (Nisbett & Ross, 1980) demonstrated how doctors might interpret a patient's symptoms in a way that aligns with their initial diagnosis, even when alternative diagnoses are plausible. This bias can delay accurate diagnoses and lead to inappropriate treatments, particularly in complex or ambiguous cases (Croskerry, 2003). In addition, anchoring bias, where clinicians fixate on an initial piece of information, can also affect clinical judgment, causing them to overlook subsequent, more relevant data. Several studies in recent years have found that cognitive biases, including confirmation and anchoring biases, were major contributors to diagnostic errors in radiology, with significant implications for patient outcomes (Graber et al., 2018; Graz et al., 2005; Thiels et al., 2015). Addressing these biases through decision support systems, structured diagnostic protocols, and reflective practices can help mitigate their impact and improve medical decision-making (Croskerry, 2003).

Electronic health records (EHRs) are the foundation of decision support systems and are important in improving patient care coordination, efficiency, and data accessibility. However, some hospitals have faced challenges with EHR implementation. Unsuccessful EHR implementations may result from inadequate planning, insufficient training, poor system usability, or resistance to change among staff members. Workflow disruptions, data entry errors, and decreased productivity can occur if EHR systems are not effectively integrated into clinical workflows or if users experience difficulties navigating and using the software. The implementation of EHRs can be critical for day-to-day operations monitoring and providing insights through further analysis of existing data, for example, by deploying AI. Reddy et al. propose that even though technological advancements and big data have only recently been put to effective use in the healthcare arena (Reddy et al., 2020). Rajpurkar et al. make this assertion and declare that "AI research has consequently blossomed in specialties that rely heavily on the interpretation of images, such as radiology, pathology, gastroenterology, and ophthalmology" (Rajpurkar et al., 2022). A substantial recent study funded by King's College London on almost 500,000 patients, where medical professionals have fed AI machines with the necessary data and collaborated to assist clinical decisions to predict stroke outcomes, has provided clear evidence that medical professionals are excellent enablers of innovative AI steps (Gilotra et al., 2023). These examples highlight the potential improvements that can still be achieved in healthcare, provided organizational insights are considered.

3.7 Challenges and Insights on How to Fix Them

As many of the challenges in healthcare are complex, the ability to address them efficiently and effectively may lie in the hands of a team rather than a single individual. Thus, team dynamics, i.e., behaviors, processes, and changes that take place within a team, become important. For example, it has been shown that team dynamics and hospital culture play a critical role in shaping healthcare outcomes by influencing communication, collaboration, and overall organizational effectiveness. Research showed that positive team dynamics, characterized by mutual respect, trust, and open communication, lead to better decision-making and improved patient care. For example, a 2015 study demonstrated that well-coordinated teams in hospitals, where leadership promotes a commitment to safety and continuous improvement, achieved fewer errors and higher patient satisfaction (Salas et al., 2015). Conversely, negative team dynamics, such as poor communication and interprofessional conflict, can undermine collaboration and compromise care quality (O'Daniel & Rosenstein, 2008). In the UK and other countries worldwide, the implementation of the "TeamSTEPPS" program in several hospitals showed improvements in teamwork, reduced medical errors, and higher patient satisfaction (Rizka Rosa & Yuanasika, 2023). Thus, a positive hospital culture that encourages transparency, inclusivity, and respect for diverse roles helps foster an environment where teams can thrive.

As healthcare is a people-driven activity, understanding people's behavior is critical. How shall such an understanding be approached? Firstly, people's health beliefs and attitudes significantly influence their health-related behaviors, decision-making processes, and treatment adherence. Understanding individuals' beliefs about health, illness, treatment efficacy, and preventive measures is crucial for healthcare providers to effectively tailor interventions and communication strategies. Cultural, social, and psychological factors also influence health beliefs and attitudes, highlighting the importance of cultural competence and patient-centered care in addressing diverse patient needs and preferences.

However, effective communication cannot be achieved without health literacy, or the ability to obtain, understand, and act on health information. Health literacy is critical in people's ability to navigate the healthcare system, make informed decisions, and manage their health. Recognizing varying levels of health literacy among patients and tailoring communication strategies accordingly is essential for promoting patient engagement, adherence to treatment plans, and shared decision-making. Finally, psychosocial factors, including emotional well-being, social support, socio-economic status, and past experiences with healthcare, profoundly impact people's healthcare experiences, satisfaction, and outcomes. Tailoring interventions and communication strategies to align with patients' health beliefs, literacy levels, and psychosocial factors fosters meaningful patient engagement, can promote adherence to treatment plans, and ultimately enhance the quality of care and patient outcomes.

References

Akinrinmade, A. O., et al. (2023). Artificial intelligence in healthcare: Perception and reality. *Cureus, 15*, 9.

Alarilla, A., et al. (2022). Why have ambulance waiting times been getting worse? *Health Found.*

Bass, B. M., & Riggio, R. E. (2006). *Transformational leadership*. Psychology Press.

Bevan, G., & Hood, C. (2006). Have targets improved performance in the English NHS? *BMJ, 332*(7538), 419–422.

Boamah, S. A., et al. (2018). Effect of transformational leadership on job satisfaction and patient safety outcomes. *Nursing Outlook, 66*(2), 180–189.

Croskerry, P. (2003). The importance of cognitive errors in diagnosis and strategies to minimize them. *Academic Medicine, 78*(8), 775–780.

Cummings, G. G., et al. (2018). Leadership styles and outcome patterns for the nursing workforce and work environment: A systematic review. *International Journal of Nursing Studies, 85*, 19–60.

Dorfman, P. W. (1996). International and cross-cultural leadership research. *Handbook for international management research, 2*(1), 504–518.

Edmondson, A. C. (2003). Framing for learning: Lessons in successful technology implementation. *California Management Review, 45*(2), 34–54.

Eldred-Evans, D., et al. (2023). The rapid assessment for prostate imaging and diagnosis (RAPID) prostate cancer diagnostic pathway. *BJU International, 131*(4), 461–470.

Frampton, A., et al. (2017). Using real-time, anonymous staff feedback to improve staff experience and engagement. *BMJ Open Quality, 6*(1), u220946–u2w7041.

Frankel, A., et al. (2005). Patient safety leadership WalkRounds™ at Partners Healthcare: Learning from implementation. *The Joint Commission Journal on Quality and Patient Safety., 31*(8), 423–437.

Gilotra, K., et al. (2023). Role of artificial intelligence and machine learning in the diagnosis of cerebrovascular disease. *Frontiers in Human Neuroscience, 17*, 1254417.

Graber, M. L., et al. (2018). Learning from tragedy: The Julia Berg story. *Diagnosis, 5*(4), 257–266.

Graz, B., et al. (2005). Prognosis or "curabo effect?": Physician prediction and patient outcome of surgery for low back pain and sciatica. *Spine, 30*(12), 1448–1452.

Johnson, A., et al. (2016). Time to change: A review of organisational culture change in health care organisations. *Journal of Organizational Effectiveness: People and Performance, 3*(3), 265–288.

Khuntia, J., et al. (2022). Valuing diversity and inclusion in health care to equip the workforce: Survey study and pathway analysis. *JMIR Formative Research, 6*(5), e34808.

Lambrou, P., Kontodimopoulos, N., & Niakas, D. (2010). Motivation and job satisfaction among medical and nursing staff in a Cyprus public general hospital. *Human Resources for Health, 8*, 1–9.

McCann, J. T., Graves, D., & Cox, L. (2014). Servant leadership, employee satisfaction, and organizational performance in rural community hospitals. *International Journal of Business and Management, 9*(10), 28.

Montgomery, A., et al. (2019). Burnout in healthcare: The case for organisational change. *BMJ, 366*.

Nisbett, R. E., & Ross, L. (1980). Human inference: Strategies and shortcomings of social judgment.

O'Daniel, M., & Rosenstein, A. H. (2008). Professional communication and team collaboration. In *Patient safety and quality: An evidence-based handbook for nurses*.

Okpala, P. (2021). Addressing power dynamics in interprofessional health care teams. *International Journal of Healthcare Management, 14*(4), 1326–1332.

Perez, J. (2021). Leadership in healthcare: Transitioning from clinical professional to healthcare leader. *Journal of Healthcare Management, 66*(4), 280–302.

Rajpurkar, P., et al. (2022). AI in health and medicine. *Nature Medicine, 28*(1), 31–38.

Reddy, S., et al. (2020). A governance model for the application of AI in health care. *Journal of the American Medical Informatics Association, 27*(3), 491–497.

Richards, A. (2020). Exploring the benefits and limitations of transactional leadership in healthcare. *Nursing Standard, 35*(12), 46–50.

Rizka Rosa, D. M., & Yuanasika, D. (2023). Team effectiveness intervention using TeamSTEPPS in healthcare: A literature review. *Jurnal Aisyah: Jurnal Ilmu Kesehatan., 8*(3).

Ryan-Fogarty, Y., O'Regan, B., & Moles, R. (2016). Greening healthcare: Systematic implementation of environmental programmes in a university teaching hospital. *Journal of Cleaner Production, 126*, 248–259.

Salas, E., et al. (2015). Understanding and improving teamwork in organizations: A scientifically based practical guide. *Human Resource Management, 54*(4), 599–622.

Sammer, C. E., et al. (2010 Jun). What is patient safety culture? A review of the literature. *Journal of Nursing Scholarship, 42*(2), 156–165.

Saw, S. N., & Ng, K. H. (2022). Current challenges of implementing artificial intelligence in medical imaging. *Physica Medica, 100*, 12–17.

Shanafelt, T. D., & Noseworthy, J. H. (2017). Executive leadership and physician well-being: Nine organizational strategies to promote engagement and reduce burnout. In *Mayo clinic proceedings* (Vol. 92, No. 1, pp. 129–146). Elsevier.

Tanrıverdi, E. Ç., et al. (2025). The road to collaboration: The transformative effects of interprofessional education on students' interprofessional attitudes and readiness, socialisation and valuing in medical and nursing students. *Nurse Education in Practice, 82*, 104230.

The Premier of Victoria, Australia. (2023). New milestone for moderna vaccine facility. Available at: https://www.premier.vic.gov.au/new-milestone-moderna-vaccine-facility

Thiels, C. A., et al. (2015). Surgical never events and contributing human factors. *Surgery, 158*(2), 515–521.

Thorlby, R., Gardner, T., & Turton, C. (2019). NHS performance and waiting times. *The Health Foundation, 22*.

Waring, J., Currie, G., & Bishop, S. (2013). A contingent approach to the organization and management of public–private partnerships: An empirical study of English health care. *Public Administration Review, 73*(2), 313–326.

West, C. P., Dyrbye, L. N., & Shanafelt, T. D. (2018). Physician burnout: Contributors, consequences and solutions. *Journal of Internal Medicine, 283*(6), 516–529.

West, M. A., Eckert, R., Steward, K., et al. (2014). *Developing collective leadership for health care*. King's Fund.

Wilson, D. K., Kaplan, R. M., & Schneiderman, L. J. (1987). Framing of decisions and selections of alternatives in health care. *Social Behaviour, 2*(1), 51–59.

Wong, C. A., Cummings, G. G., & Ducharme, L. (2013 Jul). The relationship between nursing leadership and patient outcomes: A systematic review update. *Journal of Nursing Management, 21*(5), 709–724.

Insights for Resilient and Patient-Centric Healthcare Systems

4

Liz Sparacino and Annette Schmid

Healthy citizens are the greatest asset any country can have.
—Winston Churchill

4.1 The Importance of Resilient Health Systems

Geo-political tensions, wars, natural disasters, and health emergencies in recent years illustrate the importance and potential fragility of healthcare systems in the criticality of their continuity in the face of adversity. In addition to the impact on the economy and business, the effects on human lives are disastrous. According to the WHO, over 7 million lives were lost globally due to COVID-19, with the pandemic causing significant disruptions to health services (World Health Organization, n.d.). In early 2022, the WHO reported continued COVID-19 (World Health Organization, 2020), pandemic-related disruptions of essential health services in 90% of the 129 countries surveyed; for example, in more than half of the countries, many people were still unable to access primary and community care, 36% of countries experienced significant emergency care disruptions, and 59% saw delays and cancellations of elective surgeries. Both staff and funds were reassigned from supporting noncommunicable disease services to COVID-19 (World Health Organization, 2020), resulting in avoidable illness, disability, and death as people were unable to get care for other conditions, like heart disease and diabetes. In addition to their direct impacts on people's lives, pandemics, war, and other disasters may affect healthcare centers more broadly; lead to water, energy, and medical supply shortages; and impact access to healthcare facilities when infrastructure is damaged. Travel to some healthcare facilities may become more complex and dangerous, and the demands on the medical system may

L. Sparacino
Initiative for Science & Society, Duke University, Durham, NC, USA

A. Schmid (✉)
Takeda Pharmaceuticals, Cambridge, Massachusetts, USA
e-mail: Annette.Schmid@takeda.com

B. Alknawy (ed.), *Organizational Insights: Healthcare Perspective*, Springer Series in Healthcare Management and Innovation,
https://doi.org/10.1007/978-3-032-10532-5_4

be poorly distributed, with some local regional healthcare systems overburdened while others remain underused (Ekzayez et al., 2021).

4.1.1 Patient Access to Healthcare

Even without disruptive events, travel to healthcare centers burdens patients everywhere. Depending on the health condition and location, some families need to relocate to access expert care—this is particularly prevalent in families that care for a family member living with a rare condition (Alnasser et al., 2024). Globally, most patients live at least 2 h away from tertiary care centers providing access to clinical trials (Agrawal et al., 2021). While the relationship between distance to specialized care and health outcomes is complex (Kerschbaumer et al., 2021; Kelly et al., 2016), long distances may create a significant hurdle to healthcare access for many reasons, ranging from professional or family obligations to financial costs. The lack of close access to pediatric specialized care particularly impacts developing and low-income countries (Alnasser et al., 2024).

Consider Jane Doe[1], for example: Jane is a single mom with three young children living in a remote rural area. She manages a rare gastrointestinal disorder that requires her to frequently travel over 90 min each way to see a specialist. To afford her medical needs and support her family, Jane works two jobs while juggling the care of her three children. On days when she has specialist appointments, she must take time off work, potentially losing income from both jobs, pay for transportation costs, rearrange other work and family commitments, and ensure her children are safe and cared for while she is away. Although the appointments are crucial to her well-being and long-term health outlook, Jane is forced to balance the burden on her family and finances with her health due to the three-hour round-trip travel to appointments.

There is an expectation that access to telehealth could reduce the travel burden for patients like Jane and allow for more consistent and accessible healthcare management. Other measures can also benefit patients, such as greater integration of local health facilities into specialized care and increased flexibility for individuals to manage where and when they receive healthcare. For example, broader availability for doctor visits outside of regular business hours, options to have blood drawn closer to the home or work location, and potentially having medication delivered to the home may all reduce the burden on patients. Interestingly, in one study, one provider spoke about their observation of patients being more comfortable in their homes during telehealth services, allowing patients to share more information with them (DeHart et al., 2024).

Notably, regarding acceptance of technology, such as telemedicine, and the provision of flexibility concerning time and location, discussions with patients globally revealed that individuals' basic preferences can vary greatly, and needs may change depending on their stage in life and circumstances. Every patient is unique. For

---

[1] Jane Doe is a placeholder name commonly used in the United States and the United Kingdom. This story is hypothetical and not based on a real person's story,

example, while one patient who is retired or living alone may appreciate and look forward to the human connection provided in a visit to a clinic, another, say a professional taking care of aging parents or children, experiences the time, potential cost, and coordination needed to accommodate such a visit to the clinic as a significant burden. Similarly, the perceived importance of the particular healthcare interaction, distance, and risks associated with travel to the facility may also influence the willingness to accommodate a scheduled or recommended appointment. Finally, community and cultural ties can significantly impact whether a healthcare encounter at a potentially distant tertiary clinic or a home visit/telemedicine may be preferred. Resilient healthcare systems of the future should consider this broad range of needs and build in choices for the individual on how to access their healthcare. In a world where healthcare systems need to be prepared for disruptions, we argue that agility in healthcare provision benefits patients and prepares and bolsters the system's resilience in crisis. Policies addressing inequities in healthcare access must reflect the needs of patient communities to ensure that patients can more readily incorporate healthcare services into their lives and improve health outcomes.

4.1.2 The Need for Policy

Given the sporadic, unpredictable nature of disasters, pandemics, and emergencies, tension can exist in creating health systems optimized for efficiency and resilience (Almeida, 2024). With frequently tight budgets, healthcare systems may be reluctant to invest in relationship-building across stakeholders and mitigation frameworks for unpredictable risks; when faced with the immediate needs of emergencies, there can also be a reluctance to relinquish some institutional autonomy for greater coordination. Without regional or governmental coordination, such frameworks are rarely possible (Curfman et al., 2022). As governments and policymakers strive to set frameworks that create robust, resilient healthcare systems to benefit patients and populations, technological advances may constitute an essential pillar in that endeavor.

In this chapter, we bring together industry and academic perspectives to argue that alignment of policy with technology innovation can have a significant impact on healthcare and clinical trial conduct and improve the resiliency of the system to adversity, such as health emergencies or local, regional disruption due to conflict or natural disasters.

4.2 System Flexibility with Technology

Telehealth is a broad term referring to digital technology used to deliver and improve healthcare. It typically includes a wide range of services, such as virtual consultations with doctors, specialists, and mental health professionals, remote patient monitoring, health education, use of software applications, to view lab test results, track blood sugar or blood pressure, or request refills from pharmacies (Medline Plus, n.d). While often used interchangeably, telemedicine may better describe a subset of telehealth measures focusing specifically on the clinical aspects of healthcare that employ technology to better deliver medical care from a healthcare provider to a remotely located patient. It may apply to health care professionals using information and communication technologies to exchange valid information for diagnosis, treatment, and prevention of disease and injuries, research and evaluation, and for the continuing education of health care providers (World Health Organization, 2010).

The COVID-19 pandemic accelerated the adoption and implementation of technology to facilitate remote healthcare. For example, before the COVID-19 pandemic, telemedicine visits in the United States were low, with telehealth only accounting for <1% across all age groups (Neri et al., 2022; Statista, n.d.). Critical factors responsible for the previously low utilization include regulatory restrictions, physician licensing, and reimbursement limitations (Organization for the Economic Co-operation and Development, 2023). While the availability of these technology tools predated the pandemic, the urgency to limit the risk of exposure both for patients and healthcare workers, address overburdened health systems, and broaden access for individuals in remote locations or during lockdowns created a reset in policies governing the use and adoption of the technology and paved the way for a spike in their utilization (Turner Lee et al., 2020). The necessity to adhere to recommended practices like social distancing hastened technology integration into people's daily lives and the healthcare system. In the United States, 40% of adults said they used technology in a new or different way during the pandemic (McClain et al., 2021), and in Europe, 84% of patients were using virtual health services for the first time in March 2020 (Negreiro, 2021). In France, telehealth consultations grew tenfold, jumping from 40,000 consultations in February 2020 to 4.5 million in April 2020, and the United States recorded similarly staggering growth, with Medicare fee-for-service telehealth visits rising from 840,000 to 52.7 million between 2019 and 2020 (Williams et al., 2022).

Clinical trials constitute a unique part of the healthcare system, where research in appropriately diverse and representative patient populations is essential for developing productive and safe treatments for all afflicted with a particular health condition. As treatment interventions are investigational, additional ethical considerations apply, especially around the safety of participating patients (Bierer & White, 2023). Patients participate in clinical trials for many reasons. Often, they mention a desire to advance research into finding treatments for themselves and others living with a particular condition. For some, the investigational treatment may also be the only treatment option available, and disruption of this access because of natural disasters, war, or health emergencies causes significant emotional distress and jeopardizes the continuity of their treatment, including adequate safety monitoring.

As such, there was also a pivot to telemedicine measures in clinical trials as the COVID-19 pandemic disrupted access to healthcare and healthcare centers. The decentralized clinical trial (DCT) tracker created by ClinicalTrialsArena.com reported global DCT trends in recent years. In 2016, approximately 40% of drug trials had a decentralized component. In 2019, this increased to around 65–70% of drug trials, and by 2021, 100% of drug trials had a decentralized component, according to the DCT tracker (Fultinavičiūtė et al., 2022). In one survey, 85% of respondents reported transitioning to remote or virtual visits in ongoing trials during

COVID-19. Digital data collection was the fastest decentralized component, with a 54% increase from 2020 to 2021 (Fultinavičiūtė et al., 2022), albeit not without growing concerns over patient data privacy, security, and quality. Although telemedicine remains the most frequently used decentralized component, with over 500 new drug trials in 2022, home or alternative sites remain underutilized, with just 40 new drug trials reporting the use of this component.

While the use of decentralized components in clinical trials was generally low across the globe before the pandemic, subsequent adoption rates varied globally. The DCT tracker further illustrates this point (Maragkou & Vaidya, 2022). For instance, Australia saw the most significant percentage increase from 4.4% in 2010–2016 to 16.6% in 2019–present. Other high-income countries, such as the United Kingdom, New Zealand, and Denmark, were lower at around 14% from 2019–present, the United States was at 12.1%, and France and Spain were at around 7%. Brazil grew from 1.1% to 7.4% and Japan rose from 1.6% to 3.1%. Despite a recent slight decrease in the usage of decentralized components, usage rates remain higher than prepandemic. The increased deployment of digital technology in these trials greatly furthered our understanding of the risks and challenges of introducing, using, and integrating such digital tools and a parallel proliferation of technology (Argyres et al., 2022). The pandemic created urgency, especially for pharmaceutical and biotechnology components sponsoring clinical trials. Yet, the decentralization in the context of clinical trials is often also seen as the "democratization of clinical trials" as it may bring clinical trials and advanced healthcare to underserved or geographically isolated communities.

Today's repertoire of remote and decentralized components is extensive and growing. Some of the most used tools include telemedicine, electronic consent, previsit online surveys and symptom collection, remote patient monitoring, electronic clinical outcome assessments, mobile and home healthcare, alternative-care locations, and digital endpoints. Recent data suggests that technology and decentralized and remote healthcare measures can increasingly provide alternatives that secure continuity of care in emergencies. As discussed by Ye et al. in their analysis of telehealth implications in China and other low-to-medium income countries (LMICs), the distribution of tasks and responsibilities, in addition to access to scarce expertise, can also provide relief for healthcare professionals during emergencies or times of limited resources (Ye et al., 2023). As data on the use and impact of virtual and remote solutions supporting clinical trial planning and execution is still scarce, Tufts University's Center for the Study of Drug Development (CSDD) has established a precompetitive consortium called PACT (Partnership for the Advancement of Clinical Trials) to gather and analyze hard evidence. Early insights from clinical trial sponsors and contract research organizations collaborating in the PACT consortium suggest that one-third of all protocol procedures and half of all study visits could be performed remotely in clinical trials deploying decentralized clinical trial components. Such utilization accelerates clinical trial conduct, and specific elements, such as access to specialty laboratories, may be associated with higher enrolment among diverse populations.[2]

[2] Funded in part by the Reagan-Udall Foundation. To learn more about the PACT Consortium contact Joán Chambers at joan.chambers@tufts.edu or Zak Smith at zak.smith@tufts.edu.

4.2.1 Risks to Be Considered in the Context of Technology Use in Healthcare

Health data is considered sensitive data that should be carefully managed and protected. While electronic health data can facilitate rapid transmission of data across potentially difficult terrain or long distances, all actors involved have an obligation to honor the privacy and security of the patients and avoid unauthorized access to the data that may jeopardize privacy, including inappropriate access to mental health information, diagnoses, medical history and procedures, and other sensitive information. Patients have a reasonable expectation that the conversation they have with their providers and the data that is collected about them will be accessed only by individuals with a legitimate purpose. Adequate stewardship of such data that includes protection and privacy is crucial to mitigate risks of discrimination and negative impact on employment or insurance opportunities for patients, their families, and communities. Ethical accessioning, handling, use, and sharing of sensitive health-related data is also fundamental to patient- and societal trust and to the successful adoption of technologically enhanced healthcare systems. While laws and regulations are varied and fragmented across jurisdictions, foundational and emerging protections exist.

Impact of Data Privacy Laws

Data privacy laws lay out a framework to protect health data in many regions. For example, the European Union's General Data Protection Regulation (GDPR), which by many is considered to be one of the most stringent and patient-centric regulations, includes strict data transfer restrictions, a principle of accountability, a patient's rights to access and to be "forgotten," and the right to be informed (Mishova, 2024). GDPR has had significant influence internationally, and concepts from the GDPR can also be found in numerous other international privacy laws in countries such as China, Brazil, and Japan (Mishova, 2024). In the United States, recent years have seen a dynamic landscape of emerging state privacy laws. The current key legislation relating to health data is, however, the Health Insurance Portability and Accountability Act (HIPAA) of 1996. Under HIPAA, all medical records and other identifiable health information used or disclosed by a "covered entity," whether electronically, on paper, or orally, are covered (U.S. Department of Health and Human Services, n.d.). It applies to a relatively narrow range of entities that collect, process, analyze, and transfer such "personal health information (PHI)" and constitutes data privacy protections specifically for the transfer of health data between "covered entities" like insurance companies and healthcare providers. This also applies to a patient that joins a telehealth platform for mental health services; their virtual session and associated data will be protected. Yet, other health-related data may not be covered. In today's dynamic technology sector, myriads of devices and platforms are available to consumers that collect health-related data broadly (e.g., heart rates, sleep and movement pattern). The protection of this data is sporadic and associated with risks. For example, data that a patient enters about their provider preference when creating an account on the telehealth platform is not subject to HIPAA compliance. In the case of the platform BetterHelp, such data was sold to third parties, including Facebook and Meta, without proper consent and disclosure (Federal Trade Commision, 2023).

We consider it best practice to have clear informed consent mechanisms where patients understand if their data will be shared with other providers or parties, and the risks and purposes of such sharing. Additionally, we recognize that opt-in systems for nonessential transfer of data to third parties and anonymization of data where appropriate provide additional privacy protections for patient health data.

Artificial Intelligence, Machine Learning in healthcare

In recent years, there has also been an unprecedented proliferation of technology that applies artificial intelligence (AI) and machine learning (ML) across all sectors, including healthcare (World Economic Forum, 2023; World Health Organization, 2021). AI/ML technology has promised to broaden and accelerate the technology tools discussed here and simplify the user experience with technology. If thoughtfully implemented, it may improve both the scope and accessibility of healthcare services at a global scale (Ciecierski-Holmes et al., 2022). Significantly, in LMICs or health systems under duress from disruptive events, future employment of AI/ML may contribute to local expertise and bandwidth (Zuhair et al., 2024).

Bias in Predictive Technology

It is well understood that value alignment of AI systems with shared societal values such as fairness, privacy, and justice is imperative. In addition, the risk of introducing and amplifying unconscious bias in algorithms is significant. Careful consideration of what constitute appropriate data sets to use for the training of algorithms is important. Yet, deep learning methods have opaque inner workings, which can make it difficult to predict failures. Failures do occur, however. For example, AI facial recognition technology has been shown to be less accurate for people with darker skin tones and women. Other studies found that AI systems are worse at prediction for patients of lower socioeconomic status.

Within this chapter, we do not have the scope to deeply examine the deployment of AI/ML for future health systems; however, we notice that access to well-curated, appropriately diverse, privacy-secured, and sizeable digital data is a prerequisite for robust algorithms, generalizability, and bias-mitigating insights. Governments, researchers, developers, and healthcare providers need to work together to advance adequate frameworks for the development and use of AI/ML in healthcare and minimize risks of negative impact to health outcomes, communities, and individuals.

4.2.2 Policy Alignment and Coordination

As COVID cases skyrocketed globally, policymakers quickly responded to the urgent public health demands by removing restrictions and implementing systems to enable widespread telehealth utilization.

The United States adopted a short-term strategy by issuing a Public Health Emergency (PHE) declaration to loosen regulatory requirements for Medicare telehealth services (McClain et al., 2021). Later, a myriad of loosened requirements for behavioral/mental telehealth services were permanently established, allowing Medicare patients to receive services from home, regardless of geographical location, and through audio-only platforms (U.S. Centers of Medicare and Medicaid, 2023). Eased requirements for nonbehavioral/mental telehealth services were extended to the end of 2024 by the Consolidated Appropriations Act of 2023 (US Department of Health and Human Services, 2023) but have yet to become permanent policies. India invested more funding in healthcare and launched a mandatory national tele-consultation service, and Saudi Arabia launched the National Transformation Program 2020 to integrate telehealth services into the existing system (Areeba et al., 2021). Other countries, including France and the Netherlands, similarly adjusted restrictions for teleconsultations, allowing nearly all healthcare professionals to provide teleconsultations regardless of previous visits with a patient or the technology available (Williams et al., 2022). The Health Professions Council of South Africa also removed some restrictions around telehealth, allowing a swift breakthrough in telehealth use (Dodoo et al., 2022). Other countries, including Austria, Greece, Ireland, Italy, and Malta, adopted long-term approaches by enacting legislation to allow more open use of digital health solutions like e-prescriptions (Williams et al., 2022).

Some countries took unique approaches to providing COVID services to low-density or rural areas. Kazakhstan established regional telehealth headquarters to address its widespread but low-density population distribution (Bhaskar et al., 2020), and Ghana utilized drones to deliver COVID-19 test samples (Dodoo et al., 2022). However, other countries faced significant barriers and could not implement telehealth services. One study investigating the telehealth gaps in Nigeria reported that clinicians believed safety issues such as data security and privacy, the absence of reliable internet connectivity and power, lack of awareness, and lack of financial incentives were some of the barriers to the underutilization of telemedicine in their nation (Adenuga et al., 2020).

While each country tailored its response to adopting remote healthcare technology, some countries still face barriers around technology literacy and awareness, internet access, infrastructure, and safety in integrating technology into healthcare systems.

In telemedicine and telehealth, clarity on roles and responsibilities in compliance with the local and regional laws and regulations is paramount but can be complex, especially if services extend over state or national borders. We have seen particular challenges with the decentralized healthcare provider's adequate licensing for the service recipient's location, regulatory acceptability of direct-to-patient drug supply, and secure data transmission. In the United States, telehealth poses jurisdictional and insurance challenges that may need to be understood and can be cumbersome and confusing.

If our Jane Doe was, for example, taking part in a global clinical trial where she was able to collect her buccal swab samples at home but needed to have them shipped internationally for a centralized analysis, this may require significant paperwork and if not done correctly may result in a loss of the sample. Alternatively, suppose she is a college student who has been in treatment for depression. In that case, she may be able to continue her treatment virtually with the psychiatrist she knows well and has a strong relationship with as long as she stays in the same state or country. However, if she does a semester abroad, licensing requirements may preclude her from that treatment continuation when such a safety net might be precious.

If there is a desire to create resilience in the healthcare system through digital health technology, policy alignment providing a clear framework, including resource allocation, infrastructure, and oversight, will be critical (Alnasser et al., 2024). Mitigations, such as alternative energy provision in case of power outages due to emergency disruptions or vulnerable infrastructure, should be considered (Singh, 2023). Robust broadband or cellular networks across the geography to support digital technology may need to be created (Ye et al., 2023).

In our experience, there is also a need and opportunity for coordination toward broadly used technology platforms that can securely integrate the different telehealth services and receive input from a wide range of contributing systems. Government agencies or widely accepted supranational organizations may best facilitate such coordination (Smith et al., 2020; Curfman et al., 2022). Healthcare providers commonly share concerns about having to handle too many different technology tools, such as for patient scheduling, tele-visits, and electronic health records. They may sometimes be required to use different software platforms when interacting with various regions. There are concerns about insufficient training and familiarity with the technology, combined with a lack of support, which healthcare providers frequently raise. The combined effect can be overwhelming, especially in already resource-limited conditions.

4.3 Patient Centricity and Careful Evaluation of Community Needs

As more data on the perspectives of patients and healthcare providers on a wider use of decentralized components emerges, it is clear that allowing flexibility in the approach is critical. Patients have a wide range of preferences and needs constantly shifting and evolving in their circumstances (e.g., child- and elder care, family and professional obligations, or specific medical needs).

4.3.1 Evaluation Through an Ethics of Care Approach

Ethics of care, also called care ethics, provides a unique lens through which to consider patient-centric decisions and policies that may be particularly suitable for a broad, global framework. Ethics of care as a framework is contextual and grounded in our relational and interdependent nature. It takes a broader approach by understanding the network of people, identities, and barriers involved in medical decisions with the understanding that humans do not exist in a vacuum. Consequently, policy impacts people embedded in their webs of social factors and barriers and governs decisions for individuals within the complex network of people in their lives.

While care ethics has been applied to social policy (Mahon & Robinson, 2011), further work would help expand its use in health policy. Current publications demonstrate that ethics of care in policy can be: (1) attentive to present-day needs, (2) sensitive to how power shapes and alters our relational dynamics in all stages of the policy process, (3) capable of providing a deeper understanding of the underlying forces contributing to injustices, and (4) more responsive to how health policy shapes individual's lives (Greenswag, 2019), which lends the opportunity to impact patient outcomes positively. Considering patterns of power in the policy process, Greenswag (2019) argues, "The question of who holds the greater parity of power during the policy process can be made explicit using the lens of care ethics, and how that power is used must be carefully considered to foster responsible use of power for the betterment of people and the relationships people maintain." The question of power is thought to force policymakers to understand their role in the policy process and how their perspectives shape their approach.

4.3.2 Exploring Ethics of Care in Practice

In the example of telehealth, the ethics of care lens provides insight into how telehealth may impact families. For example, in more individualistic societies, measures ensuring broad access to telehealth may need to be supplemented with technology support for individuals who live alone and may not be fully technology literate. Ethics of care may also inform policy in regions where multigenerational households are more common. Here, too, care ethics would promote careful consideration of how telehealth policies impact the patient, their living condition, and the potential impact on other family members living in a household by exploring technology support needs and availability, the implication for the individual providing the support, and societal expectations.

Through a care ethics lens, policymakers might then explore with the communities to what extent policy solutions such as technology-support hotlines or brochures might be beneficial. A care ethics lens would also encourage policymakers to consider how telehealth impacts the power dynamics between providers and patients. Some patients and providers state that telehealth can eliminate the unsettling feeling of an unfamiliar, potential doctor's office. Accordingly, some patients and caregivers may feel more comfortable and empowered using telehealth technology in their homes (DeHart et al., 2024), while others may not want to share the circumstances they live in. Ethics of care can influence policy by providing insight into relationships, power, context, care, and other nuances that more traditional policy processes may not capture.

4.3.3 The Patient Experience with Healthcare Technology

As mentioned previously in this chapter, access to healthcare can be limited, complex, and dangerous in the context of disruptions from health emergencies, conflicts, or natural disasters. The practical implications of accommodating visits to treatment facilities in the context of other commitments and obligations such as work, families, and community responsibilities can also create barriers. In our work, common feedback from patient advisory boards suggests that flexibility in the type of access is critical to eliminating the burden for patients. Families and patients from the rare disease community, patients with rare diseases, and those living with chronic conditions highlight the convenience of technology that reduces travel (Tahsin et al., 2024). Yet, at times, patients may also appreciate the more substantial experience of care and community that in-person interactions with treatment teams bring. Some individuals may appreciate the sense of safety and quality of care that direct treatment team engagement and the clinical environment may bring. National circumstances and cultural preferences add further nuance to the broad range of patient preferences and illustrate the importance of providing opportunities to patients and caregivers to voice their preferences and, ideally, to be able to make choices.

Further, data from pediatric studies at Children's Hospital Sant Joan de Deu in Barcelona illustrates that what we think as healthcare providers may not always be what caregivers and patients prefer (Claverol, 2023). Whereas families saw particular benefits in the ability to conduct simple tests at home, treatment teams at clinical sites voiced reservations (Claverol, 2023). Like families with children that need sustained support from treatment teams (Curfman et al., 2022), time commitment related to treatment and monitoring, stigma (Obisike, 2018), and practical challenges to regular visits with healthcare teams can be significant for adults living with chronic conditions (Sayani et al., 2019).

4.3.4 Prospective and Sustained Community Engagement

To develop culturally appropriate healthcare systems, we recommend co-creating the policy framework with representatives of the regional communities, especially those from underrepresented or vulnerable communities. Today, it is well understood that this engagement ought to occur early and sustainably. In industry, we may engage in consortia-style collaborations to foster and participate in such engagements. For example, the UK-based Paddington Life Science Partners[3] are working closely with community leaders in the culturally and ethnically highly diverse Northwest London to understand the unique needs of this highly transitory population and develop better access to health care, including culturally feasible and acceptable enabling technology solutions. Paddington Life Science Partners is setting a leading example of community engagement by hosting round table discussions within community spaces, ensuring that research is of value to relevant communities, and seeking to understand better how to engage local communities in research by surveying them directly. Understanding the fundamental values and concerns of the various communities in a particular catchment area will be critical

[3] Paddington Life Science Partners https://www.imperial.nhs.uk/paddington-life-sciences/about-us/our-difference.

to frame the parameters, accommodate individual preferences, and provide the flexibility ranges needed once the system goes live.

Co-creation with community leaders with cultural humility is not only the right thing to do (U.S. Centers for Disease Control and Prevention, n.d.), it also increases the likelihood of acceptance and adoption of innovative systems and may create essential champions in their intended communities (Redvers et al., 2024).

In the public sector, government officials may engage communities at various levels, for example, they may host round table discussions to get insight into patient perspectives and consult the public via online platforms, interviews, etc., to effectively engage all stakeholders in the policy process that are affected by or affect policy. Internationally, engaging stakeholders in policy helps policymakers understand the differences between groups in communities, creates more socially responsive and practical policy, builds consensus, and increases transparency (Idriss-Wheeler et al., 2024). It can also help avoid unintended consequences of policy, generate more policy options and solutions, increase public understanding, and highlight problems with existing policies. When the necessary voices are included in the policy-making process, it helps ensure that policy is effective for the communities it ultimately impacts, ensuring that patient needs are met. In contrast, it should be well understood that when provided feedback is not sufficiently considered, it will be perceived as tokenistic (Masefield et al., 2021).

Consider Jane Doe again. Recall that Jane is living in a remote rural area. Local government officials hosted a round-table discussion, and Jane and a range of other residents attended to listen to updates on policy changes to a regional health clinic. Jane explains that in conversation with her neighbors, she noticed that residents felt the current hours of the clinic could not meet their needs. Her neighbors mentioned that due to long work commutes into the city, they could not utilize the regional health clinic's free or reduced-cost health services. This is due to a recent growth in a nearby city that has led to more residents in her town commuting for work rather than working locally. At the round table, Jane brings up this conversation with her local government officials, who were unaware of the recent increase in commuting to work. The local government officials decided to conduct a regional study to understand new barriers that arise with a high percentage of residents commuting to work and survey residents to understand better what hours at the clinic may best serve their community. Without the inclusion of community members like Jane, her town may have overlooked a critical barrier in attending to local patient needs and an opportunity to improve health outcomes.

4.4 Emerging Insights on Resilient Healthcare Centers and Their Providers

Healthcare system resilience has the potential to profoundly affect patient satisfaction, trust, and overall societal well-being. Medical needs create a unique vulnerability and perceived dependence, which is heightened during disrupted or uncertain access to services. Patients, their families, and caregivers are often acutely aware of risks discontinuation of care and lack of access will bring and value efforts of reliable, uninterrupted, high-quality health access and effective care coordination. However, if the route to access is disrupted and/or the levels of quality of care and indeed the trustworthiness of the institution or care provider are low, patients and their families will not seek the acute, recurrent, or preventative care, often with detrimental effects to their well-being and public health. Potentially, overwhelmed by the circumstance and the complexity of receiving care, continuity of care not only provides an anchor of normalcy but also a lifeline for continued and/or future health.

In dermatology, the advantages of connecting specialist providers to remote or underserved areas are well documented. For example, the Alaska Federal Health Care Access Network (AFHCAN) in the United States is a successful telehealth initiative where teledermatology is an active component. This network connects over 700 providers across more than 250 sites, many of which are clinics serving remote populations without access to the road system, significantly broadening access in a geographically challenging region. India's telemedicine initiative by the Indian Space Research Organization (ISRO) provides connectivity to nearly 60 remote hospitals, which are connected with 20 specialty city hospitals for teleconsultation and treatment. These remote hospitals act as clinics or healthcare centers in underserved areas, bolstered with access to specialist dermatological input through teledermatology. The Australian New South Wales Telehealth Initiative serves a variety of sites, including aboriginal settlements and nursing homes. These can be considered as local healthcare access points benefiting from teledermatology consultations, thus broadening access for these communities. The Africa Teledermatology project collaborates with numerous public and private organizations that provide healthcare throughout Africa, including hospitals and clinics. Through their web-based platform, they provide teledermatology consultation services to local physicians and healthcare workers in these facilities, expanding access to dermatological expertise in resource-limited settings. Over 700 consultations have been submitted from over twelve African countries, indicating active use by clinics in these regions (Desai et al., 2010).

A study in Saudi Arabia compared the diagnoses and management plans of face-to-face consultation with those made by a second dermatologist viewing images taken with a mobile phone and reported broad categorical diagnostic and management and found good agreement with a concordance (95%) and an average kappa coefficient of 0.66 for diagnostic concordance and 0.82 for management concordance. Importantly, this study also assessed patient satisfaction with the mobile teledermatology consultation using a questionnaire. Most responding patients were highly satisfied with teledermatology, but 23 out of 166 patients (14%) refused photography of their skin lesions. The majority of these patients were women with lesions on the face and chest. The authors hypothesized cultural sensitivities (Kaliyadan et al., 2013).

Cultural sensitivities may at times also favor the use of technology as results from the use of mobile telemedicine for the diagnosis and/or triage of cervical precancer/cancerous lesions and skin disease in HIV-infected patients in Botswana suggested. Skin diseases are common in Botswana and morbidity can be significant. Often, these conditions are unique to or present more severely in HIV-infected patients than in the nonimmunosuppressed population. A severe lack of dermatologists in the region means long journeys to specialist clinics for those affected, unless community centers are connected via telemedicine. It also appears that the stigma of cervical cancer and HIV may add further reluctance toward seeking specialist care that can be mitigated if images can be captured privately and submitted (Azfar et al., 2011).

Limited studies focus on the provider's unique perspective on the impact of the streamlined adoption of telemedicine.

In one example, a pre-COVID study explored healthcare provider benefits from telehealth in rural communities in a southeastern US state where rural healthcare providers may spend significant time traveling between offices to provide care to their communities (DeHart et al., 2022). Implementing telehealth reduced the travel burden, allowing providers to see more patients and patients to access care more efficiently. Another study examining the perspective of 17 providers across 11 different organizations in South Carolina, United States, highlighted that even when providers had prior experience with telehealth, they still expressed feelings of crisis and faced challenges in scaling up technology to meet the needs implicated by the pandemic. A publication co-authored by the Ghana Health Service also speaks to the importance of early engagement of healthcare workers in the development phase and the provision of adequate training on the new technology (Labrique et al., 2018). In a successful campaign, they were able to mobilize the utilization of mobile phones by community health workers in remote communities and districts. The researchers consider the user-based design a critical success factor in promoting sustained uptake and use. The switch to mobile-enabled telemedicine services allowed a nationwide roll-out in Ghana, providing measurable benefits to the health system, including reductions in unnecessary hospital referrals.

A study in Israel revealed that telemedicine during the COVID-19 lockdown led to a 3.5% rise in primary care visits with a 5% reduction in per-episode cost, thus slightly lowering the overall resource utilization. Importantly, remote visits resulted in fewer prescriptions with no evidence of missed diagnosis or adverse outcomes reported in follow-up visits (Zeltzer et al., 2024). Careful road-testing and monitoring of such implementations in the region of interest will be necessary as a US cohort study from 2019–2022 suggested that in a high volume and high-stress setting of the pandemic, telehealth may have provided greater ease of access to more interactions, but the quality of this care may have been lower as it was associated with a larger number of subsequent acute or chronic health issues that led to potentially preventable hospitalizations and higher overall health care costs (Saharkhiz et al., 2024).

4.5 Ensuring Future Successful Technology and Policy Alignment in Healthcare Systems

4.5.1 Affordability and Practicality of Technology

In recent years, more data has become available on the challenges and opportunities of telehealth in low-to-medium income countries (LMICs) such as China (Ye et al., 2023), India (Singh, 2023), and Sub-Saharan Africa (Alnasser et al., 2024), highlighting many potential benefits from improved access to specialist healthcare in LMICs to reductions in travel cost and income sacrifices, improved health outcomes such as increased quality-adjusted life years, opportunities to mitigate language and cultural barriers, to workload redistribution and educational support for providers (Alnasser et al., 2024). However, what are the broader systems implications? The setup cost of software applications, training, and the more comprehensive infrastructure of the technology can be expensive if it is not preexisting. To be resilient, including in the face of natural disasters or regional conflicts, careful planning for backup energy, such as solar power, enabling the technology may also be necessary (Singh, 2023). Data on direct cost and return on investment for setting up a resilient, technology-driven system is mixed, with most resources suggesting a long-term benefit (Alnasser et al., 2024). On the practical side, misaligned priorities and interests among stakeholders can hamper successful implementation (Ye et al., 2023). Unfamiliarity with a system can create barriers to the adoption of telehealth by providers and patient communities.

Consequently, mobile health via smartphones may present a more penetrative alternative for young people while utilizing existing resources. In China, one study found that telemedicine was most commonly used for remote consultation and that a popular application (app) called WeChat was the most common technology (Ye et al., 2023). By using an already widely available and utilized app, China minimized barriers to telemedicine. Other countries may find other communication and social media networks more suitable for their communities. This builds upon the idea that smartphones and existing technology can be utilized, particularly in LMICs, to support telemedicine while potentially limiting additional financial or resource burdens as long as the privacy of the information is secured.

4.5.2 Our Recommendations

Throughout this chapter, we have laid the groundwork for three essential principles to ensure technology and policy alignment is effective and successful and betters patient outcomes in the communities it functions in: (1) foster co-creation within and across communities, (2) promote the coordination of simple, practical health systems, and (3) create agile systems that accommodate variable patients and community needs.

Foster Co-creation Within and Across Communities

Above, we made the case that resilient and effective policy must be carefully crafted according to community/patient needs and values. Susan Edgman-Levitan and Stephen C. Schoenbaum (2021) speak powerfully to this notion: "Whatever form it takes, changing the focus from taking unilateral action to improve health and healthcare for the people to taking action with the people is simple yet radical." In our experience, policy cannot be for the people or help the people it serves unless it deeply considers people's needs and values in the drafting, development, and usage. We believe that the broad outlines of health policy should be discussed and ideally co-created with community leaders to lay the groundwork for community awareness and culturally acceptable frameworks that effectively align policy with the potential of innovative technology. The unique context of their history needs to be understood to address and mitigate potential past injustice or systemic marginalization. For true agility, communities and healthcare providers should be prepared and accepting of integration before the time of emergency. Here, ethics of care can provide a lens to policy that focuses on the context, power dynamics, and relationships that a community relies on. Given the technology use proposed here, infrastructure that contains adequate safeguards on cybersecurity and patient privacy protection will need to be developed and maintained to foster societal trust in the platforms and shield patients from the risk of discrimination and injury to reputation or welfare. When governments set the standard that health policy is community-focused, it establishes trust in communities and reliable systems to continue engaging communities, creating resilience in emergencies and pandemics.

Promote the Coordination of Simple, Integrated Health Systems

Health systems across the globe are resource-limited. Commonly, health systems must carefully balance infrastructure investment, staffing, and staffing time management. While there is great promise in technology to aid and streamline healthcare, the cost of quality technology is not trivial, and healthcare workers have limited capacity to learn the use of new technology platforms and accommodate new processes and workstreams. It is impractical for healthcare workers to use many technology platforms with various logins and user interfaces. When systems are not integrated, the potential need to enter some of the same data multiple times into different technology platforms can add to the cumbersome experience and increase the risk of data entry errors. Data and technology standards may hasten and enable such integration. To realize the ambition of resilient healthcare systems with technology, we should strive for coordination toward a few well-integrated technology platforms that are interoperable with multisource data compatibility. Building on or emulating the look and feel of widely available social media platforms could be beneficial for greater end-user ease and adoption. If these technology platforms are in place and in use in advance of disruptive events, they can provide opportunities for health systems to swiftly and efficiently adapt technology and policy to meet evolving health needs.

Create Agile Systems That Accommodate Patients and Communities

Finally, if implemented thoughtfully, we believe we can create resilient access to healthcare that is flexible enough to accommodate our populations' wide-ranging and changing preferences. Such an approach could secure the ability for all to seek the healthcare services they need in their day-to-day lives by reducing some of the burdens that distance to healthcare providers and scheduling constraints may bring, thus strengthening a critical pillar of population health. Importantly, however, a system that provides greater flexibility to patients in where, when, and how to access healthcare services can also be more agile in response to disruptive events, such as future pandemics, natural disasters, and conflicts, and can be a strong foundation for resilient healthcare systems of the future.

We thank Zisis Kozlakidis, Missy Heidelberg, Maximillian Evans-Schmid, Ting Shih, and Karine Sargsyan for their input and editorial advice.

References

Adenuga, K. I., Iahad, N. A., & Miskon, S. (2020). Telemedicine system: Service adoption and implementation issues in Nigeria. *Indian Journal of Science and Technology, 13*(12), 1321–1327.

Agrawal, G., Xue, J., Moss, R., Raschke, R., & Wurzer, S. (2021). No place like home? Stepping up the decentralization of clinical trials. *McKinsey.* https://www.mckinsey.com/industries/life-sciences/our-insights/no-place-like-home-stepping-up-the-decentralization-of-clinical-trials

Almeida, A. (2024). The trade-off between health system resiliency and efficiency: Evidence from COVID-19 in European regions. *European Journal of Health Economics, 25*, 31–47.

Alnasser, Y., Proaño, A., Loock, C., Chuo, J., & Gilman, R. H. (2024). Telemedicine and pediatric care in rural and remote areas of middle-and-low-income countries: Narrative review. *Journal of Epidemiology and Global Health, 14*(3), 779–786. https://doi.org/10.1007/s44197-024-00214-8

Areeba, T., Asif, O., Khadim Arain, F., & Munir, M. W. (2021). COVID-19 compels medical practitioners and governments to promote telemedicine practices. *Applied Medical Informatics, 43*(2), 68–80. https://orcid.org/0000-0001-6480-0064

Argyres, D., Hung, A., Kennedy, K., Pérez, L., & Tolub, G. (2022) Digital health: An opportunity to advance health equity. *McKinsey.* https://www.mckinsey.com/industries/life-sciences/our-insights/digital-health-an-opportunity-to-advance-health-equity#/

Azfar, R. S., Weinberg, J. L., Cavric, G., Lee-Keltner, I. A., Bilker, W. B., Gelfand, J. M., & Kovarik, C. L. (2011). HIV-positive patients in Botswana state that mobile teledermatology is an acceptable method for receiving dermatology care. *Journal of Telemedicine and Telecare, 17*(6), 338–340.

Bhaskar, S., Bradley, S., Chattu, V. K., Adisesh, A., Nurtazina, A., Kyrykbayeva, S., Sakhamuri, S., Yaya, S., Sunil, T., Thomas, P., Mucci, V., Moguilner, S., Isreal-Korn, S., Alacapa, J., Mishra, A., Pandya, S., Schroeder, S., Atreja, A., Banach, M., & Ray, D. (2020). Telemedicine across the globe-position paper from the COVID-19 Pandemic Health System Resilience PROGRAM (REPROGRAM) International Consortium (Part 1). *Frontier Public Health, 8.* https://doi.org/10.3389/fpubh.2020.556720

Bierer, B., & White, S. A. (2023). Ethical considerations in decentralized clinical trials. *Bioethical Inquiry, 20*, 711–718.

Ciecierski-Holmes, T., Singh, R., Axt, M., Brenner, S., & Barteit, S. (2022). Artificial intelligence for strengthening healthcare systems in low- and middle-income countries: A systematic scoping review. *npj Digit Med, 5*(1), 162. https://doi.org/10.1038/s41746-022-00700-y

Claverol, J. (2023). Unpublished presentation at Annual IMI Trials@Home conference, October 2023.

Curfman, A., Hackell, J. M., Herendeen, N. E., Alexander, J., Marcin, J. P., Moskowitz, W. B., Bodnar, C. E. F., Simon, H. K., & McSwain, S. D. (2022). Telehealth: Opportunities to improve access, quality, and cost in pediatric care. *Pediatrics, 149*(3), e2021056035.

DeHart, D., Iachini, A. L., Browne, T., Reitmeier, M., & King, L. B. (2024). Telehealth use during COVID-19: An exploratory study on adaptations and experiences of providers. *Health and Social Work, 49*(2), 95–104. https://doi.org/10.1093/hsw/hlae001

DeHart, D., King, L. B., Iachini, A. L., Browne, T., & Reitmeier, M. (2022). Benefits and challenges of implementing telehealth in rural settings: A mixed-methods study of behavioral medicine providers. *Health & Social Work, 47*(1). https://doi.org/10.1093/hsw/hlab036

Desai, B., McKoy, K., & Kovarik, C. (2010). Overview of international teledermatology. *Pan African Medical Journal, 6*(3).

Dodoo, J. E., AI-Samarraie, H., & Alsswey, A. (2022). The development of telemedicine programs in Sub-Saharan Africa: Progress and associated challenges. *Health and Technology, 12*, 33–46. https://doi.org/10.1007/s12553-021-00626-7

Edgman-Levitan, S., & Schoenbaum, S. C. (2021). Patient-centered care: Achieving higher quality by designing care through the patient's eyes. *Israel Journal of Health Policy Research, 10*(21), 4. https://doi.org/10.1186/s13584-021-00459-9

Ekzayez, A., Alha Ahmad, Y., Alhaleb, H., & Checchi, F. (2021). The impact of armed conflict on utilisation of health services in north-west Syria: An observational study. *Conflict and Health, 15*, 91. https://doi.org/10.1186/s13031-021-00429-7

Federal Trade Commission. (2023). *Complaint: In the matter of BetterHelp, Inc., before Commissioners Lina M. Khan (Chair), Rebecca Kelly Slaughter, and Alvaro M. Bedoya.* Retrieved November 22, 2025, from https://www.ftc.gov/system/files/ftc_gov/pdf/2023169-betterhelp-complaint_.pdf

Fultinavičiūtė, U., Maragkou, I., Castañeda, R., & Hillman, A. (2022). DCT Tracker: Tracing industry's adoption of decentralised clinical trials. *Clinical Trials Arena Verdict Media Limited.* https://www.clinicaltrialsarena.com/features/dct-adoption-tracker-who-and-what-is-at-the-crest-of-the-trial-decentralisation-wave/

Greenswag, K. (2019). Care ethics and public policy: A holistic, transformative approach. *Politics & Gender, 15*(4), 912–940. https://doi.org/10.1017/S1743923X18000521

Idriss-Wheeler, D., Ormel, I., Assefa, M., Rab, F., Angelakis, C., Yaya, S., & Sohani, S. (2024). Engaging community health workers (CHWs) in Africa: Lessons from the Canadian Red Cross supported programs. *PLOS Global Public Health, 4*(1). https://doi.org/10.1371/journal.pgph.0002799

Kaliyadan, F., Amin, T. T., Kuruvilla, J., & al Bu Ali, W. H. (2013). Mobile teledermatology - Patient satisfaction, diagnostic and management concordance and factors affection patient refusal to participate in Saudi Arabia. *Journal of Telemedicine and Telecare, 0*, 1–5.

Kelly, C., Hulme, C., Farragher, T., & Clarke, G. (2016). Are differences in travel time or distance to healthcare for adults in global north countries associated with an impact on health outcomes? A systematic review. *BMJ Open, 6*, e01305. https://doi.org/10.1136/bmjopen-2016-013059

Kerschbaumer, J., Freyschlag, C. F., Bauer, R., Obwegeser, A. A., Schubert, G. A., Thomé, C., & Seiz, M. (2021). Distance to the neurooncological center: A negative prognostic factor in patients with Glioblastoma Multiforme. An epidemiological study. *Anticancer Research, 32*, 5515–5520.

Labrique, A. B., Wadhwani, C., Williams, K. A., Lamptey, P., Hesp, C., Luk, R., & Aerts, A. (2018). Best practices in scaling digital health in low and middle income countries. *Global Health, 14*, 103. https://doi.org/10.1186/s12992-018-0424-z

Mahon, R., & Robinson, F. (2011). Introduction. In *Feminist ethics and social policy: Towards a new global political economy of care.* University of British Columbia Press. https://doi.org/10.59962/9780774821070

Maragkou, I., & Vaidya, M. (2022). DCT tracker: Charting the next chapter for decentralization. Last updated in August 2024. *Clinical Trials Arena.* Retrieved September 16, 2025, from https://www.clinicaltrialsarena.com/features/dct-adoption-tracker-who-and-what-is-at-the-crest-of-the-trial-decentralisation-wave/?cf-view

Masefield, S. C., Msosa, A., Chinguwo, F. K., & Grugel, J. (2021). Stakeholder engagement in the health policy process in a low-income country: A qualitative study of stakeholder perceptions of the challenges to effective inclusion in Malawi. *BMC Health Services Research, 21*, 984. https://doi.org/10.1186/s12913-021-07016-9

McClain, C., Vogels, E. A., Perrin, A., Sechopoulos, S., & Rainie, L. (2021). The Internet and the Pandemic. *Pew Research Center.* https://www.pewresearch.org/internet/2021/09/01/the-internet-and-the-pandemic/

Medline Plus. (n.d.). *What is telehealth?* Retrieved February 6, 2024, from https://medlineplus.gov/telehealth.html

Mishova, A. (2024). Global Data Protection Regulation: How GDPR sets the international standard. *GDPR Local.* https://gdprlocal.com/global-data-protection-regulation-how-gdpr-sets-the-international-standard/

Negreiro, M. (2021). The rise of digital health technologies during the pandemic. *European Parliamentary Research Service (briefing).* https://www.europarl.europa.eu/RegData/etudes/BRIE/2021/690548/EPRS_BRI(2021)690548_EN.pdf

Neri, A. J., Whitfield, G. P., Umeakunne, E. T., Hall, J. E., DeFrances, C. J., Shah, A. B., Sandhu, P. K., Demeke, H. B., Board, A. R., Iqbal, N. J., Martinez, K., Harris, A. M., & Strona, F. V. (2022). Telehealth and public health practice in the United States - Before, during, and after the COVID-19 pandemic. *Journal of Public Health Management & Practice, 28*(6), 650–656. https://doi.org/10.1097/PHH.0000000000001563

Obisike, E. E. (2018). The effectiveness of telemedicine on stigmatization and treatment burden in patients with health compromising lifestyles and chronic diseases: A critically appraised topic. *Open Science Journal, 3*(1). https://doi.org/10.23954/osj.v3i1.1413

Organization for the Economic Co-operation and Development (OECD). (2023). *The future of telemedicine after COVID-19.* https://www.oecd.org/content/dam/oecd/en/publications/reports/2023/01/the-future-of-telemedicine-after-covid-19_3b64f3d8/d46e9a02-en.pdf

Redvers, N., Odugleh-Kolev, A., Cordero, J. P., Zerwas, F., Zitoun, N. M., Kamalabadi, Y. M., Stevens, A., Nagasivam, A., Cheh, P., Callon, E., Aparicio-Reyes, K., & Kubota, S. (2024). Relational community engagement within health interventions at varied outcome scales. *PLOS Global Public Health, 4*(6). https://doi.org/10.1371/journal.pgph.0003193

Saharkhiz, M., Rao, T., Parker-Lue, S., Borelli, S., Johnson, K., & Cataife, G. (2024). Telehealth expansion and Medicare beneficiaries' care quality and access. *JAMA Network Open, 7*(5). https://doi.org/10.1001/jamanetworkopen.2024.11006

Sayani, S., Muzammil, M., Saleh, K., Muqeet, A., Zaidi, F., & Shaikh, T. (2019). Addressing cost and time barriers in chronic disease management through telemedicine: An exploratory research in select low and middle-income countries. *Therapeutic Advances in Chronic Disease, 10*, 1–10. https://doi.org/10.1177/2040622319891587

Singh, J. (2023). The COVID-19 pandemic: An opportunity to strengthen telemedicine in low and middle-income countries. *Pediatric Research, 93*, 463–464.

Smith, A. C., Thomas, E., Snoswell, C. L., Haydon, H., Mehrotra, A., Clemensen, J., & Caffery, L. J. (2020). Telehealth for global emergencies: Implications for coronavirus disease 2019 (COVID-19). *Journal of Telemedicine and Telecare, 26*(5), 309–313. https://doi.org/10.1177/1357633X20916567

Statista. (n.d.). *Telemedicine use before and after COVID-19 in the U.S., by age.* Retrieved February 5, 2024, from https://www.statista.com/statistics/1234973/telemedicine-use-before-and-after-covid-19-in-the-us-by-age/

Tahsin, F., Bahr, T., Shaw, J., Shachak, A., & Steele Gray, C. (2024). The relationship between treatment burden and the use of telehealth technologies among patients with chronic conditions: A scoping review. *Health Policy and Technology, 13*(2), 100855. https://doi.org/10.1016/j.hlpt.2024.100855

Turner Lee, N., Karsten, J., & Roberts J. (2020). Removing regulatory barriers to telehealth before and after COVID-19. *The Brookings Institute.* https://www.brookings.edu/articles/removing-regulatory-barriers-to-telehealth-before-and-after-covid-19/

U.S. Centers for Disease Control and Prevention. (n.d.). Embracing cultural humility and community engagement: Global health equity. *CDC.* Retrieved September 15, 2025, from https://restoredcdc.org/www.cdc.gov/global-health-equity/php/publications/cultural-humility.html

U.S. Centers for Medicare & Medicaid Services. (2023). *Coverage to care: Telehealth providers: What you need to know.* U.S. Department of Health and Human Services. Retrieved February 6, 2024, from https://www.cms.gov/files/document/telehealth-toolkit-providers.pdf

U.S. Department of Health & Human Services. (2023). Telehealth policy changes after the COVID-19 public health emergency. *Telehealth Policy Updates.* Retrieved February 6, 2024, from https://telehealth.hhs.gov/providers/telehealth-policy/policy-changes-after-the-covid-19-public-health-emergency

U.S. Department of Health & Human Services. (n.d.). *Summary of the HIPAA Privacy Rule.* Retrieved November 22, 2025, from https://www.hhs.gov/hipaa/for-professionals/privacy/laws-regulations/index.html

Williams, G. A., Fahy, N., Aissat, D., Lenormand, M.-C., Stuewe, L., Zablit-Schmidt, I., Delafuys, S., Le Douarin, Y.-M., & Azzopardi Muscat, N. (2022). COVID-19 and the use of digital health tools: Opportunity amid crisis that could transform health care delivery. *Eurohealth, 28*(1) https://iris.who.int/bitstream/handle/10665/351081/Eurohealth-28-1-29-34-eng.pdf

World Economic Forum. (2023). Scaling smart solutions with AI in health: Unlocking impact on high potential use cases. *World Economic Forum with ZS*. https://www3.weforum.org/docs/WEF_Scaling_Smart_Solutions_with_AI_in_Health_Unlocking_Impact_on_High_Potential_Use_Cases.pdf

World Health Organization. (2010). *Telemedicine: Opportunities and developments in member states: Report on the second global survey on eHealth*. Retrieved February 6, 2024, from https://iris.who.int/handle/10665/44497

World Health Organization. (2020). *The impact of the COVID-19 pandemic on noncommunicable disease resources and service: Results of a rapid assessment*. Retrieved February 6, 2024, from https://iris.who.int/bitstream/handle/10665/334136/9789240010291-eng.pdf?sequence=1

World Health Organization. (2021). WHO issues first global report on artificial intelligence (AI) in health and six guiding principles for its design and use. *WHO News Release*. https://www.who.int/news/item/28-06-2021-who-issues-first-global-report-on-ai-in-health-and-six-guiding-principles-for-its-design-and-use

World Health Organization. (n.d.). *WHO Coronavirus (COVID-10) dashboard cases*. Retrieved February 5, 2024, from https://data.who.int/dashboards/covid19/cases

Ye, J., He, L., & Beestrum, M. (2023). Implications for implementation and adoption of telehealth in developing countries: A systematic review of China's practices and experiences. *npj Digital Medicine, 6*, 174. https://doi.org/10.1038/s41746-023-00908-6

Zeltzer, D., Einav, L., Rashba, J., & Balicer, R. D. (2024). The impact of increased access to telemedicine. *Journal of the European Economic Association, 22*(2), 712–750. https://doi.org/10.1093/jeea/jvad035

Zuhair, V., Babar, A., Ali, R., Oduoye, M. O., Noor, Z., Chris, K., Okon, I. I., & Rehman, L. U. (2024). Exploring the impact of artificial intelligence on global health and enhancing healthcare in developing nations. *Journal of Primary Care & Community Health, 15*, 21501319241245847. https://doi.org/10.1177/21501319241245847

Future Perspective Insights: Healthcare and Medical Sciences

5

Karine Sargsyan

5.1 Introduction

New organizational specificities in the healthcare sector and medical sciences introduce significant challenges to ensure that the strategy and implementation of considered planning and coordination of hospitals, clinical laboratories, diagnostic centers, and bio-resources meet the demand and needs of the final users and payers. According to Filip et al. (2022), this chapter presents some of the identified organizational peculiarities in the healthcare and medical sciences sector. For instance, what resources an organization needs and what type of internal structures or strategies must be developed to support such development. It shows that knowledge and technology management are highly relevant to organizations today, principally in health and medicine. According to De Bem Machado et al. (2022), the main contribution is the intensification of the use and measure of the impact of knowledge and intellectual capital management in future healthcare and medical organizations. The basic model has shown the dynamics of such organizations. Emphasis on the health sector's organization and the dire need for designing a complex and modern organizational structure of hospitals, laboratories, and other medical organizations. All these fall under the scope of the contemporary economic perspective. In this regard, Dahiyat et al. (2023) argue that the unique features attributed to healthcare organizations from a modern economic perspective. The following section exceptionally elaborates on different aspects of organizational specificities, supplemented by an

K. Sargsyan (✉)
IBD Institute and OncoBiobank, Cedars-Sinai Medical Center, Los Angeles, CA, USA

International Biobanking and Education, Medical University of Graz, Graz, Austria

Department of Digital Medicine and AI and Department of Medical Genetics, Yerevan State Medical University, Yerevan, Armenia
e-mail: Karine.Sargsyan@cshs.org

B. Alknawy (ed.), *Organizational Insights: Healthcare Perspective*, Springer Series in Healthcare Management and Innovation,
https://doi.org/10.1007/978-3-032-10532-5_5

enlightened analysis of the complexities involved in the performance and diagnostics of medical research. In the end, there is a conclusive section to summarize the discussion and evidence presented and draw conclusive remarks summarizing the whole discourse regarding the subject matter (Barr, 2023; Bolden et al., 2023).

In the ever-evolving environment that characterizes today's healthcare, it is important to examine even the minute details that define organizations' very base. Where an organization requires resources to grow or evolve, structure and strategies that could present an avenue for such growth or development from within must be considered. Knowledge and technology management are the basis for most organizational success, especially in broader health and medical care areas.

It is a voluminous work because it has been able to put up many ways to measure the intensity of the changes that knowledge and intellectual capital management unleash on future healthcare and medical organizations. The underlying principles of a dynamic model of such organizations, which can turn around the operational work and take it to dizzy heights, can also be found in the deeper channels of this exploration (Ozgun et al., 2022). Looking from the perspective of the healthcare sector organization, it becomes crystal clear that there is an urgent need for a modern and advanced framework. Hospitals, laboratories, and other health centers are looking for innovative approaches to match the ever-evolving demand from the modern economic perspective. This chapter discusses the typical features supporting this idea of exploration. We note that several aspects combine to form the quirks of organizational dynamics. We conduct an astute analysis as the entwining tapestry of medical research performance and diagnostics is unwoven. This is meant to enlighten us on specifics beneath the surface that provide clarity and newness of unprecedented vision regarding this multifaceted realm (Munoz-Gama et al., 2022).

We are expected to work toward those key results that conclude this organizational-rational journey of preparing for future demands. We need to summarize comprehensive knowledge gained in significant subject matter. With each word written and explored, another horizon comes into view and beckons us onward, further to unravel the mysteries waiting to be unfolded (Munoz-Gama et al., 2022).

5.1.1 Background and Rationale for the Future of Healthcare Organization

The aspects discussed are well reflected in the literature on health economics, healthcare management, and economic psychology literature on organizational peculiarities as an integrative concept of healthcare reforms, management of healthcare institutions, microeconomic interactions between providers and patients, and interpretation of sector-specific manner to evaluate private and public goods provided by healthcare organizations (Shi & Singh, 2022; Cleverley et al., 2023). While this finding is not disparaged, many other phenomena and notions of difference characterize the influence of such organizational curiosities. For instance, the so-called third-party demanders received universal acceptance for describing the role of health insurance organizations or the government that finances and collects taxes for this purpose on behalf of the first-party healthcare consumers and second-party healthcare providers. However, in all positive analyses of healthcare systems' organization and healthcare policy coordination, it was always emphasized that not only the design of health insurance systems but even the rights and duties of providers and patients themselves and, even more so, the distribution of institutional needs and authority as such appear to create institutional specificities.

The same applies to a property relation. Since the government, in general, predominantly acts as the property owner. Resources are allocated for the public needs of society, and thus, in the healthcare system in particular, this fact determines the institutional environment for providers and the relations between them. The ability and intent to act productively, generate profits, create organizational and technological novelties, organize and elicit employees' intrinsic or extrinsic motivation, or treat their patients individually and in a patient-friendly way depend, too, on the prevailing property relations and governance system. The underpinnings of performance improvements and health cost savings may support the increasing importance of corporate health management, healthcare quality management, and other modern organizational principles and tools within these organizations.

Such are the following current problem solutions: (a) realization of protection of consumer rights as an engine of regulation and legal health consumer rights protection at the national, regional, or international levels; (b) competitive regulation, competition institutionalization, including dual competition and jurisdiction enforcement on transboundary markets and the struggle against illegal and unlicensed activities; (c) certification and licensing of healthcare organizations, professionals, appliances, devices, and drugs as a means of improving comparability and confidence. There are specific reasons why, in healthcare, these standard tools developed concerning defined criteria should be further institutionalized by establishing more sophisticated fourth-party and fifth-party demanders. (d) Healthcare consumer protection associations and counselling centers or independent accreditation, inspection, and approval bodies might represent the latter. Moreover, (e) due to the continuous intensity of growth and the controversial distribution of individual and social benefits to the health sector and its services, the demand for social responsibility of healthcare organizations and healthcare professionals appears to be an issue of vital importance (Ferlie & Ongaro, 2022; Nilsen et al., 2020).

5.2 Understanding Organizational Peculiarities of Future Planning in Healthcare

Healthcare management supervises and administers organizations and institutions that focus on offering the desired and quality health services. In comparison with other domains of management, health service delivery possesses some peculiar features that make it unique. Some of these features include inelastic demand, with a positive sloping curve, which shows that the demand for care is always reasonably constant regardless of price or supply variations (Neelima et al., 2024). It also possesses a unique meaning for consumers and providers within healthcare; the former requires the latter to manufacture and provide the necessary care. Healthcare delivery "involves" joint production; this means the concurrent creation and consumption of different components comprising products, services, interactions, and institutional environments (Dion & Evans, 2024). It involves a complicated process whereby coordination and proper handling must be ensured if the services rendered are to be effective and productive. Historically, healthcare organizations were managed by some form of superior entity under a landlord employer, and strategic viewpoints had to incorporate statutory obligations. Professionals within organizations usually have direct links with the church due to the historical and spiritual roots of healthcare provision. Concerning the health and medical sciences field, there has arisen a dire need to formulate and ascertain communication networks owing to the complexity and specialty of service delivery. Accordingly, proper management of horizontal communication among people of the same level in the management hierarchy of the hospital will enable cooperation and coordination.

Similarly, vertical communication is also required effectively from the hospital's top management to all professionals for the coherent and efficient development and operation of healthcare services. Through the instigation of open and transparent communication, health organizations ensure that all the healthcare team members work toward the common objective of providing quality medical treatment-related services for the diversified needs of the patients (Junaid et al., 2022).

The particular dynamics of the healthcare industry and the quest to provide quality care have resulted in the development of an organizational theory peculiar to the industry, with its founders and seminal events, and a management approach that addresses nursing specifically, having its framework of operations. As significant are the market inefficiencies created by the asymmetry of information and imperfect competition within the healthcare industry itself.

5.2.1 Structural Characteristics

Our view of healthcare as a "distinctive" organization is placed within a "socio-spatial" perspective. It is an idea of a socio-spatial perspective, which acknowledges healthcare's unique institutional reorganizations. Digging deeper into the distinctive features, we focus on the "socio-spatial" structural dimensions that define health as having a particular identity. Many examples in health support the features of a distinctive organization (Junaid et al., 2022). One such example involves addressing the aging issue, which concerns the organization. This is characteristic of only a handful of private enterprises, where only a few social and healthcare entities lead the pack in actively retaining employees beyond 50 (Junaid et al., 2022). These initiatives for older employees also further differentiate the organization. In this way, like any other investment, they are auxiliary to some larger developmental schema. Organizations will benefit from marginal savings on direct personnel costs as labor becomes more productive through investment in these internal measures. The effect of the measures diffuses beyond the organization's boundary. Externally, this will also lead to increased scrutiny and gratification by both clients and consumers (Amedari & Ejidike, 2021). Through these, focusing on the welfare and retention of older workers, the organization, in turn, gains a good image with the society in which they operate. Conclusion The strategy to address healthcare as a unique entity has had an innate understanding of its socio-spatial dimensions. Understanding the distinctive profile of this particular population and taking steps toward its retention will make health organizations more effective and less costly. This will help the organization to build a good reputation.

5.3 Challenges and Opportunities in Healthcare Organizations in the Near Future

These ideas offer insight into several organizational issues on some researchers' healthcare agenda. These ideas are not directly concerned with healthcare and general medical science domains but are of specific interest to family therapy. As technical changes in the organization's design are vital, they should not be a superficial shield for more profound social and political concerns. Junaid et al. (2022) point out that, on the one hand, the conflicts between primary and specialist practice attract significant interest in the practice organization. Anyways, it is necessary to value the critical contribution of both practices toward the work in the medical field. The rising interest in single-handed practice suggests multifaceted workforce distribution topics in the system, not a fundamental shift in structure. However, other significant changes in the medical world have massive importance, too. There are competent staff who can deliver extended roles in the care of patients but are tied and responsible to the noble medical profession. In whatever manner the medical profession might be reconstructed, it retains much of its conventional authority over crucial decisions about medical needs. This is organizational research in this area that underlines the attention to be paid to the complex and meaningful elements of the individual, the team, and the personal world of the dedicated carer that inform the identity and role of healthcare professionals. These cannot be left to the mercy of the organization within which the professionals ply their noble craft.

5.3.1 Technological Advancements

Nowadays, we are living in the new wave of using technology: big data, data analytics, artificial intelligence (AI), and robot technology support decision-makers in hospitals or any other healthcare settings to reach their decisions. This urges rapid progress backed by large corporations that have entered the industry to invest in and benefit from healthcare projects. Examples of crucial health data achievements include but are not limited to electronic health records, genomics, telemedicine, home monitoring, personalized medicine, computer-aided discovery and design, machine learning prediction, healthcare mobile technologies, patient online communities, nanotechnology, and brain simulation. Alowais et al. (2023) explain that wearable technologies, remote monitoring, devices, and further development in implant technologies are creating opportunities that will bring better care to patients, monitor them outside of hospitals, help them stay at home, and rescue them with early interventions that make the difference in saving their lives.

These are not issues that are likely to disappear, and it is not a challenge to which technology alone can find the solution. There remains ample opportunity for technology to play a significant role in dealing with the mentioned obstacles and challenges and for technology companies that can deliver better metrics to benefit from them. Though AI will replace hazardous, repetitive tasks in the industry, the number one goal of new tech in healthcare would be to keep patients alive. Another vital piece of advice on the future outlook has been the capability of AI-enabled services to scan health-related information at lightning speed. Furthermore, health professionals think that AI capabilities will accelerate regular office tasks, expedite decision-making, and bring efficiency to operations (Tasheva & Karpovich, 2024).

5.4 Impact of Organizational Specifics on Patient Care

Within organizational peculiarities in healthcare and medical sciences, there are hypotheses concerning their influence on patient care and how they can be resolved. Organizational peculiarities include shortages in medical staff in some specialties, a high burden of aged patients, predicted activities of hospitals, and so on. Even if the individual peculiarities are ironed out and then the organizational peculiarities in their entirety, the positive effects of both might not accumulate. Another worthwhile aspect in which the effect takes center stage relates to medical students getting tuned to the learning curve of the two-relationship structure. The care to be instituted for a limitation of specialist doctors or other limitations is to be made transparent so that they can consider their position and the relationships of independence with them (De Vries et al., 2023).

In seeking the request for patient-centered care that minimizes error and maximizes safety in actual practice, increasing attention is given to the importance of the educational process in developing the relationship between patients and physicians in future physicians. The following are new hypotheses of the learning curve and the crucial role of internal medicine courses as clinical clerkships for first-year medical students (Li & Wong, 2023). Proposed positive promotion effects include respect for the patient, mission, acquisition of communication skills between a patient and a provider, and tendencies of first-year medical students' empowerment. It has been possible for a program in the internal medicine course to improve the relationship between the patient and physician as a starting role in the education system to date. They are crucial elements in maintaining the enthusiasm of individuals and hence play a facilitating role in the persistence of patient-centered medicine training in a patient-physician relationship (Wu et al., 2022). As a fundamental element, such forecast methods also provide knowledge and possible tasks to react to. The established influences of two-relationship educational models have brought current care practices. To increase the number of involved students and maintain the high care outcomes in healthcare and medical sciences, administration, indicators, and privacy respect may be reconsidered with concrete methods. More importantly, the significance of and future perspective on the learning curve of potential problems can also be gauged (Cottingham et al., 2022).

5.5 Future Directions and Innovations

Future healthcare and medical sciences need a holistic, multidisciplinary approach to organizational settings. An urgent requirement for more robust tools and comprehensive techniques for modeling and understanding the most complex organizational situations is at hand. Restructuring existing management sciences is a must, independently or in conjunction with various other disciplines. It requires ordinary travel adaptation resilience and flexibility toward continuous change, the dynamic health environment, and medical sciences. Together, we can help build a world where health is the force for transformation that touches and aspires to improve people's and society's lives. We should get going with this mission on solid will and determination, knowing our contribution towards this would go a long way in making healthcare more inclusive, compassionate, and innovative (Subrahmanya et al., 2022).

5.5.1 Artificial Intelligence in Healthcare

Whereas the coronavirus epidemic is the perfect example, healthcare will soon focus on preventing disease and monitoring a person's health before illness. That means instead of treatment of the sick, it will focus on not becoming ill in the first place. Many innovations, gadgets, and technological solutions cannot help but impact the healthcare system and bring more connectivity into an individual's approach. Data from wearable sensory technologies used in healthcare likely form the basis of disease prevention, diagnosis, and treatment. Innovation and better decision-making are valued more than traditional or enduring practices by the new generation of medical professionals (see Chap. 4).

5.5.2 Other Technological Advances

In this progressive era in the history of health development, it has been clear that significant technological changes have been at the forefront in introducing these unparalleled times. Health, accepted as the foundation upon which humanity based its cooperation and progress, has sparked the application of sciences related to medicine in healthcare. The landscape has been reconstituted, and many barriers have been torn down through telemedicine and fixed cameras in operation and consulting rooms, making education, training, and medical extension valid across borders. In addition, balanced resource distribution reached a new dimension with operational convergence, where medical services may be operated under different roofs or within the same roof to assure safety and efficiency at maximum levels (Khan & Khan, 2023; Omaghomi et al. 2024).

Parnell and Lester's work has been the foundation of modern health units and health clusters, allowing surgical and medical specialties to work hand in hand to achieve advances that are almost as incredible. Segmentation of space within healthcare units could be conceptualized to provide a fruitful route toward the research and development valleys or health districts, forming industry-university and university-hospital links of real value. It is necessary to highlight that healthcare organizations' peculiarities reflect the development of industries that took part in the ever-growing pursuit of becoming advanced. According to the work of Gottumukkala et al., experiences are often drawn from unforeseen events. Challenges Faced and Overcome Often, such experiences show striking similarities and require only a broader lens, an inspiring objective, and a more comprehensive approach concerning educational systems designed to produce professionals embracing the noble cause of healthcare and medical sciences. This has been considered fundamentally necessary in a world that undergoes constant metamorphosis to accommodate cultures, patients, and diseases of all types. The encouragement of integration in the middle of such formative changes is rewarding, regardless of whether or not significant outbreaks make us reconsider such a vital aspect of social and economic life (Wiedermann et al., 2023).

Much has been achieved so far, and even more is to come. However, it is essential to remember that no matter how miraculous the medical and surgical tools may become, they can never replace the invaluable intelligence and commitment a human being provides. In light of this, we stand at the threshold and ask whether we are about to embark on an actual digital revolution in healthcare.

Layers of healthcare institution-specific organizational: Features of collaboration and cooperation can be researched at various levels of the healthcare organization structure. Three of them are considered the most sophisticated and given the exact specifics of the healthcare field a patient and their characteristic malfunction is the final recipient of any organizational decisions in the healthcare setting, where all subprocesses are to align to the trusted path to that atom of the results. In this case, they do not follow a patient through the most leveraged hierarchical level but follow the theoretical formal objectives of the hierarchy building. Potent innovations and practical implementations related to any organizational design must demonstrate their ability to facilitate the circulation of detailed and back-casted information, within an intelligent, self-regulated ecosystem across different layers of the leading supplier of patient survival resources and healthcare settings. In a modern health institution, this must be a system linking information needs and information available in real-time mode. Thus, the patient would be the unique embryo wherein the ecology of processes-molecules would work. As already mentioned above, the following most important profile is that of the organizational setting and structure (Al-Jaroodi et al., 2020).

The human potential as the key to success: The staff are the unique interoperational links between the hospital administrators and the patients. The abilities and characteristics of health workers, the unique nonsymbolic translation link between organizational strategy and patient throughput, are the basics of almost all conceptual models and terminologies in addressing specific healthcare specificities with large-scale healthcare organizations modeling. Any treatment, prevention, and restoration in healthcare is confirmed according to agreed standards in coordinated subunits of healthcare, considering the increasing number of talented healthcare workers has just begun to grow. Enterprise structures can decline irrespective of hierarchical sections and reduce themselves to hiring. It could have the same result as the service professional crossing standardized stages of patient throughput in a megastructure. This is the goal: standard business units performing exceptional standard services that an average patient throughput solution cannot (Huynh, 2020; Hermsen et al., 2024; Guillari et al., 2024).

Standard operating procedures for addressing organizational specificities of future challenges: The operational complications within healthcare and medical organizations have specific natures. Thereby, custom decision-making considerations must be pursued. Organizational sustainability requires adherence to standard operating procedures. Hence, standard operating procedures at the organization that cater to the needs of healthcare management solutions and are oriented toward an outcome are of utmost importance. A study presented common standard operating procedures for identifying organizational unique characteristics and their solution (Ajegbile et al., 2024).

The future of medical practice will be based on the prevention of new emerging diseases. Still, the current global health situation will follow up on an individual's prepathological stage. The medicine of tomorrow will not focus on treating the ill but will rely on maintaining good health. The spurt in innovation, devices, and technology treatments promises a metamorphosis in medical science. The traditional system of fragmented healthcare gets its version of revolution. Technology will weave it into an integrated solution for everyone (Sargsyan, 2023). Wearable sensory technologies are expected to become the backbone of future prevention, diagnosis, and treatment. This emerging cohort is driven more by the need for innovation and informed decision-making rather than traditional and age-old Standard Operating Procedures (SOPs).

As is indicated in healthcare literature, the universe in which medical organizations live is unique, with some functioning aspects akin to the nonprofit sector while retaining all the trappings of the market (Gee et al., 2023). This holds specific implications for analysis or managerial strategies adopted in this domain. Every organization, be it medical or healthcare, might have unique features that differentiate it from other organizations of the same sector and the general concept of the domain itself. Previous studies have contended that formal education through university-level economics or medical administration is the best method for teaching business theories and practices. However, it is finally the actual application of the theories and practices that apply to the nuances of healthcare and medical organizations that serve to address and diminish critique.

Although there is some resistance to the idea, the lack of a focused and unvarying methodology in developing healthcare or medical organizations has its peculiar drawbacks. In this light, recommendations based on significant evidence seem more applicable.

One cannot be prepared for all future developments, but it is possible to analyze possible progress and prepare healthcare organizations for potential future developments. Herein, we offer actions and concrete steps to prepare a healthcare organization for future challenges (see the graph) (Fig. 5.1).

Step 1: First, an organization should focus on a detailed implementation plan to appropriately deal with future advancements in healthcare. Manifold strategies and tactics should be considered to determine how best to adapt quickly to the changing times of healthcare. Fully aware of the challenges that lie possibly ahead, efficiently analyzing those that could translate into opportunities will improve its position for its future path.

Step 2: Within the implementation plan, the steps that would smoothly adapt to changing technologies, innovations, and medical breakthroughs must be marked and outlined. It is aware of the latest developments in healthcare, prepared for what it promises, and timely integrates it into routine practice. An organization can advance technologically and use new technology to improve the patient's results and overall efficiency.

Step 3: Plan in detail a step-by-step plan for using the process at each level; this gives a methodical approach that maximizes effectiveness. The process needs to be accurately charted at each level, mapping out possible pitfalls and obstacles and plotting fallback positions.

A roadmap will help efficiently implement the process; bottlenecks will be seen from afar, and procedures will be adjusted whenever necessary to facilitate smooth progress.

Step 4: Strategic partnerships, research at the forefront of the healthcare industry, and an in-depth exploration into professional knowledge all warrant much success

Fig. 5.1 The actions and concrete steps to prepare a healthcare organization for future challenges

in the same field. Organizations will have opportunities to network with influential organizations for knowledge and resource sharing and keep up with advancements continuously molded into society. Further, investing in research and listening to experts enable it to contribute toward the growth of healthcare as a sector in general.

Step 5: Organizations' innovation and commitment to providing quality medical and healthcare services. This implies constant watch and appraisal, adjusting courses as necessary. Such dedication toward innovation and quality would promise the best treatment for the patients while keeping the organization abreast of changes in the healthcare industry now and in the future.

5.6 Conclusion and Recommendations

5.6.1 Global Recommendations and Detailed Implementation Roadmap for Healthcare Digitalization

Recommendations for Healthcare Executives: Steps to Implement AI Responsibly.

To place AI responsibly in global health systems, executives must cope with ethics, multicultural staffs, and tech gap by geography. These are steps that are seen to place AI's work in patient care in the framework of cultural, economic, and infrastructure variances in the broader world.

Establish a Global AI Ethics Framework

Healthcare executives must prioritize the creation of a culturally inclusive AI ethics framework to guide AI deployment across diverse global contexts. This involves forming a multinational ethics committee with representatives from Sub-Saharan Africa, South Asia, Latin America, and Eastern Europe to ensure AI tools align with local values, such as communal decision-making in African societies, family-centric care in Asian cultures, or individual autonomy in Western nations. The framework should mandate transparent AI models, where decision-making processes are auditable and explainable to patients and providers, particularly in low-resource settings where trust in technology may be limited. Examples are those in which rural India or remote Pacific islands are targeted by executives so that low-cost, open-source AI systems will be used for the diagnosis, hence ensuring affordability and accessibility. Ethics audits should be regularly conducted every 3 months to assess AI's impact on patient outcomes and cultural acceptance, where other matters of concern might be data bias or unintended damage. This approach builds trust and ensures compliance with international ethical standards, fostering global collaboration (Topol, 2019).

Upskill Workforce across Borders

A much-needed program for executives is the creation of broad multilingual training programs to prepare health workers worldwide for AI implications, addressing areas of disparity within education and technology familiarity. These programs should be modular, covering AI basics, data interpretation, and patient communication, and tailored to regional contexts—such as basic digital literacy for rural African nurses or advanced AI analytics for urban European doctors. Collaborations with local, national, governmental, and international organizations, such as the World Health Organization and regional health NGOs, should be put in place by the very same executives to ensure the presence of these trainings even in the most underserved areas. For instance, in Latin America, training could target the role of AI in telemedicine for remote communities, while in Southeast Asia, training can be on the tracing of infectious diseases. Executives should also establish mentorship programs pairing tech-savvy younger professionals with veteran clinicians to bridge generational gaps, particularly in aging populations like Japan or Germany. Continuous education, updated biannually, will keep staff abreast of AI advancements, enhancing their confidence and reducing resistance to technological change (Alowais et al., 2023).

Secure Data with Global Standards

Continuous fund improvements enable organizations to achieve AI readiness in different circumstances and form a basis for worldwide scaling. Hybrid cloud and offline storage systems can provide data security and tackle infrastructure issues in areas with limited connectivity, such as remote Central Asia and the Sub-Saharan Africa countryside. An example is a system of storing patient records with the help of encrypted USB drives in an area with poor internet connection and syncing to a central repository when the connection becomes available. Executives should also invest in staff training on data privacy, emphasizing cultural sensitivities around data sharing—such as reluctance in Middle Eastern cultures to disclose personal health information. Regular penetration testing and collaboration with global cybersecurity firms can preempt breaches, while anonymized datasets for AI training minimize privacy risks. This approach ensures trust and compliance, which is critical in regions with historical mistrust of medical systems, like postcolonial Latin America (Kruse et al., 2017).

Pilot AI with Regional Customization

To ensure relevance, AI would need region-specific pilot programs to be initiated by executives focusing on local health agendas, be it malaria detection in Africa, diabetes management in the Middle East, or mental health support in Europe. With open-source AI platforms adaptable to indigenous languages and datasets, costs would be reduced and pooled with collaboration beyond borders. For instance, a pilot in rural Brazil could test AI-driven telemedicine for maternal health, while one in urban China could focus on AI triage in overcrowded hospitals. Pilots should be evaluated using locally relevant metrics—community health improvements in low-income areas and hospital efficiency in high-income ones—and involve community feedback to ensure cultural alignment. Executives must continually fund improvements based on pilot evidence to support scaling without compromising quality. This method enables organizations to test AI under different circumstances and forms a basis for worldwide scaling (Subrahmanya et al., 2022).

Recommendations for Policymakers: Inclusive Frameworks to Regulate Emerging Healthcare Technologies Policymakers must develop flexible, inclusive regulatory frameworks to govern AI, telemedicine, and wearables, ensuring equitable access and safety across global healthcare systems, from resource-rich to resource-constrained nations.

Develop Adaptive Global Regulations
Policymakers should create technology-neutral regulations that evolve with innovations, drawing inspiration from frameworks like the EU's AI Act but simplified for adoption in developing nations. A UN-led global task force could standardize safety and efficacy benchmarks for technologies like AI diagnostics or wearable monitors, ensuring they meet diverse needs—such as infectious disease tracking in Africa or chronic care in aging Asia. Regulations must be designed to be flexible enough to permit local adaptation, for example, lenient data storage standards in low-infrastructure regions within minimum standards. Periodic updating of the policy based on worldwide health data can refresh regulations without suppressing innovation and still protect patients. Such coordination mechanisms build strong pillars for pandemics and global health emergencies around the world (Meskó & Topol, 2023).

Engage Diverse Global Stakeholders
"Inclusive platforms are vital for deliberation to ensure policies reflect the needs of all," from urban elites in North America to indigenous communities in Oceania. Policymakers should host regional forums involving patients, providers, tech developers, and marginalized groups—like rural health workers in South Asia or Aboriginal healers in Australia—to address challenges like last-mile connectivity or cultural resistance to telemedicine. For example, the voices of African community leaders could be used in mobile health app programming in local languages. Such forums should occur biannually, and results should be disseminated in many languages to build trust. By ensuring equity is policymakers' focus, differences can be reduced to include technology, not just for the wealthiest regions (Fatumo et al., 2022).

Strengthen Ethical Oversight Globally
Policymakers must establish regional ethics boards under a global umbrella organization, like the WHO, to monitor technology deployment, focusing on issues like AI bias against ethnic minorities or gender disparities in health data (World Health Organization, 2021). For instance, boards could investigate whether AI misdiagnoses conditions in African women due to underrepresentation in training datasets. Periodic, compulsory annual reports of transparency in local languages ensure accountability, particularly in such mistrustful historic regions, that is, post-apartheid South Africa. The boards will also develop ethical advisory guidelines concerning such new technologies as brain-computer interfaces to ensure their actions are based on the maxims of beneficence and justice. This kind of oversight creates public trust that will inspire culture-wide technology adoption.

This oversight fosters public confidence, encouraging technology adoption across cultures (Obermeyer et al., 2019).

Promote Equitable Innovation Incentives
To ensure innovations reach all regions, policymakers should offer tiered incentives—grants for low-income countries to develop affordable wearables, like low-cost glucose monitors for South Asia, and tax breaks for high-income nations investing in AI research. International trade bodies can enable technology transfer agreements to share advancements, such as telemedicine platforms, with developing countries at significant cost reductions. For example, a program could sponsor solar-powered health kiosks in rural Africa that integrate AI diagnostics with local needs. Successful models could then be promoted annually in a yearly innovation summit. This approach bridges the global technology gap, enhancing health equity (Haleem et al., 2022).

Recommendations for Researchers: Priority Areas for Future Studies in Healthcare Digitalization.

Researchers must address universal digitalization challenges while exploring region-specific nuances, ensuring findings are globally applicable yet locally relevant and supported by rigorous empirical studies.

Study AI Bias Across Diverse Populations
Researchers should investigate how AI models perform across ethnic, linguistic, and socioeconomic groups, particularly in understudied regions like Central Asia or indigenous Latin America, to prevent misdiagnoses due to biased datasets. For example, studies could explore whether AI misinterprets tuberculosis symptoms in Pacific Islander populations due to genetic diversity. Possible answers are the building of inclusive, multilingual repositories of data and the testing of AI in diverse clinical settings. Longitudinal studies, 5–10 years, can assess the impact of AI on health equity and guide global standards. These studies are essential for equitably securing AI for all populations (Rajkomar et al., 2018).

Explore Human–AI Collaboration Models
The research aims to maximize AI's complementary role with clinicians in as wide a variety of environments as possible, from Singapore's cutting-edge hospitals to rural Ethiopian mobile clinics. Research might study how AI-augmented diagnosis influences nurses' job satisfaction in Europe or patient trust in Latin America, creating frameworks that maintain human judgment while taking advantage of the efficiency of AI. Mixed-methods approaches, combining surveys and ethnographic observation, can uncover cultural barriers to collaboration, like resistance to AI in traditionalist communities. Findings should inform training programs, ensuring AI enhances, not replaces, human expertise globally (Davenport & Kalakota, 2019).

Evaluate Wearable Technologies Globally
Researchers should assess wearables' effectiveness for preventive care across diverse climates and lifestyles, such as the arid Middle East or monsoon-affected

South Asia, focusing on affordability and cultural acceptance. For instance, studies can test whether smartwatches improve blood pressure control in African urban slums through a combination of data and Indigenous healing in Indigenous settings. Randomized controlled trials for 2–3 years can validate results, and cost-effectiveness analyses ensure scalability in low-income settings.

This research will guide equitable wearable deployment globally (Dunn et al., 2018).

Investigate Digital Literacy Disparities
Research should explore barriers to digital literacy among rural, elderly, or low-income populations, developing scalable interventions like community-based training in local languages. For example, studies may quantify telemedicine adoption among older Europeans or mobile health app usage among rural Indians, reporting cultural or infrastructural barriers. Participatory action research involving the communities themselves in designing solutions can guarantee practicability and longitudinal studies track uptake rates over time. These findings will enhance patient engagement and technology uptake worldwide (Tavakoly Sany et al., 2020).

Practical Implementation Roadmap for Healthcare Organizations Globally
Above the graph and explanation given as advice in the "Technological Advances," some other ideas or parts of a roadmap can help constitute the customized and phased, globally inclusive approach to digitalization, addressing infrastructure and cultural and regulatory diversity across healthcare systems.

Technology choices must navigate disparities—cloud-based AI in Singapore versus offline solutions in rural Nigeria. Open-source platforms, like OpenMRS for EHRs, reduce costs for low-income regions, while compliance with local laws (e.g., Brazil's LGPD and China's Cybersecurity Law) ensures legal viability. Engaging local vendors fosters trust, which is critical in culturally sensitive regions like the Middle East, where foreign technologies may face skepticism. For example, voice-based AI could support illiterate populations in South Asia, while wearable integration suits tech-savvy urban Australia. Quarterly to biannual vendor reviews and pilot recommendations ensure technology alignment with regional agenda, building blocks for piloting success.

Actions:

- Evaluate technologies for cultural sensitivity, cost-benefit, and interoperability, for example, multilingual AI interfaces, as high priorities.
- Collaborate with global and local vendors to develop pilots, such as telemedicine in rural Africa or AI diagnostics in urban Asia.
- Conduct legal and cultural reviews to ensure compliance with regional data laws and societal norms.

Deliverables can be a global technology portfolio with region-specific pilot proposals (Al-Jaroodi et al., 2020).

The Regional Pilot Implementation is the next critical step, with the objective of testing technology in diverse settings to validate its efficacy and cultural fit. Pilots address unique challenges—cultural resistance in conservative Gulf states, connectivity issues in remote Amazonian villages, or regulatory hurdles in Europe. Small-scale testing builds trust, which is critical in communities wary of medical systems, like Indigenous groups in Canada. For instance, a pilot in rural Kenya could test solar-powered AI kiosks for malaria screening, while one in Germany could trial AI triage in emergency rooms. Multilingual training and hotlines operating 24/7 correct technical problems, and feedback for tool refinement is given by community forums. Scalability is steered by local indicators such as improved tuberculosis cases in Asia or increased patient satisfaction in Europe, and pilot results in feedback loops back into the worldwide strategy.

Actions:

- Launch pilots in varied contexts, like AI diagnostics in Latin American cities or wearables in African villages.
- Provide multilingual training and real-time support to ensure usability across education levels.
- Collect qualitative and quantitative feedback via surveys, interviews, and community meetings to adapt technologies.

Deliverables can be for regional pilot reports with scalability recommendations and lessons learned (Munoz-Gama et al., 2022).

The next step from here should be a global deployment and integration effort, with the objective of scaling successful technologies seamlessly across diverse healthcare systems.

The deployment must integrate with varied workflows, such as paper-based in rural Pakistan and fully digital in South Korea. Community campaigns tailored to local languages and cultural norms address skepticism, vital in postcolonial regions like Africa or Indigenous Australia. For example, radio campaigns in Swahili could promote telemedicine in East Africa, while social media drives adoption in urban Brazil. Ongoing training via mobile apps ensures accessibility for rural providers, particularly in aging populations like Italy. Interoperability with local systems, like linking wearables to India's Ayushman Bharat database, maximizes impact. Biannual evaluations ensure technologies work and global health equity becomes real.

Actions:

- Roll out technologies globally, ensuring integration with local systems like community health databases.
- Develop multilingual training apps and online portals for continuous staff education.
- Launch culturally tailored campaigns, like videos or radio spots, highlighting benefits like cost savings or improved access.

Deliverables can be a global digital ecosystem with localized user guides and support networks (Khan & Khan, 2023).

The next step should be continuous global evaluation and, if fit, innovation with the objective of sustaining digitalization through iterative improvements and global collaboration. Long-term success requires adapting to societal shifts—urbanization in Africa, aging in Europe, or pandemics globally. Use technology everywhere, in a locally integrated manner, in infrastructure such as community health registries.

Use Multilingual Applications and Web Portals to Train Workers Continuously

Tracking systems measure varied outputs, like health equity for poor nations or efficiency for wealthy nations, using dashboards with transparency obligations in multiple languages. University collaborative partnerships in Asia, Africa, and elsewhere spur innovation, such as inventions like blockchain for secure health records. Biennial refreshers address new challenges such as AI bias or cyberattacks in tech-saturated areas such as East Asia. Yearly summits highlight successes such as using AI to screen for cancer in India, which is to be adopted worldwide. This stage roots digitalization in organizational culture to guarantee robustness and inclusivity.

Actions:

- Implement a global monitoring system with (multi)lingual boards that can track outcomes like equity and efficiency.
- Foster cross-border research partnerships to explore innovations like AI-driven precision medicine.
- Update technologies biannually to address biases, security risks, and new health challenges.

Deliverables can be, for example, an annual global impact report and an innovation pipeline for future technologies (Javaid, et al. 2023).

This critical view fully elaborates the immense significance and manifold future potentials of diverse organizational capabilities of future/foresight in practice within healthcare and medical sciences. Unusual situations that are inextricably linked to operational services related to healthcare do call for an acquired and practical use of different organizational patterns that can aptly appeal to the diverse needs and expectations emanating from this sector. One of the many organizational complexities staring into the healthcare sky is the compelling need for workforce diversity. This burgeoning health sector has to have a diverse, inclusive, and culturally competent workforce to deliver the best services possible to a heterogeneous patient population (Ahmed & Adams, 2023; Williams et al., 2024). Besides this more significant pool of skill and expertise that comes with diverse backgrounds, healthcare professionals themselves can enhance the overall quality of care provided. A second critical organizational complexity involves flexibility in a healthcare setting (Haleem et al., 2022).

As healthcare delivery always carries some level of unpredictability, flexibility should be at the heart of responses on the part of healthcare organizations towards sudden challenges and abrupt changes in demand and other conditions. This flexibility should also extend to the mobilization of resources and the deployment of services in a responsive fashion. The other strange organizational complexity that defines the healthcare domain is the endless presence of high frontline and backline workloads and responsibilities. Professionals in healthcare are under immense pressure; their work is very demanding and requires relentless efforts to ensure quality patient care safely and timely. The relentless pursuit of excellence requires robust support systems, savvy task delegation, and the implementation of efficient workflows for the well-being and job satisfaction that prevent burnout among healthcare providers. This is an indispensable intricacy in healthcare as an organization provides round-the-clock services.

Healthcare professionals work tirelessly to serve the needs of medical patients who require immediate attention. Such dedication and commitment to work must be acknowledged and saluted beyond measure since continuous health service delivery implies unrivalled vigilance and response because its end is to assure optimal patient outcomes. Another organizational complexity that an organization, such as healthcare services, cannot do without involves complex and dynamic natures in the service. The nature of health organizations is that they operate at an unprecedented speed in a fast-evolving ecosystem nowadays, which requires innovative strategies, cutting-edge technologies, and professional competencies among health professionals that should be continuously developed.

The second essential organizational complexity faced by most healthcare organizations globally is the paradigm of digitalization. With the incorporation of digital technologies, electronic health records, telemedicine, and artificial intelligence, the delivery and management of healthcare services have been transformed fully. It can improve patient outcomes, expand efficiency, and make processes smoother and highly interconnected among different entities (Haleem et al., 2022). Ethical issues are among the most essential organizational complexities within healthcare. Health professionals are mandated to maintain the highest standards of ethics in providing service to patients. Ethical dilemmas arise rather often, and to meet such situations, health organizations have to set up sound frameworks, develop ethical competencies on the part of the staff, and make their way through the tangled web of moral choices so that care provided is suited to patient autonomy, justice, beneficence, and nonmaleficence. Other insightful organizational entanglements severely affecting health professionals in everyday practice include health engagement, compassion fatigue, and occupational stress (Fatumo et al., 2022). Healthcare engagement at the organizational level will be highly instrumental for cultural development in patient-centered care, empowerment among healthcare professionals, and active involvement in decision-making.

Besides this, compassion fatigue—a state of emotional, mental, and physical exhaustion that can be contextualized as an extraction of persistent exposure to others' suffering occupational stress—regularly hits practitioners in the healthcare field. Evidence-based interventions and support mechanisms should be instituted and provided to protect these committed professionals' mental and emotional welfare. It must be remembered that such organizational complexities are by no means unaware of the shaping through distinct employment statuses in a healthcare context, which includes medical doctors and nurses (Constantinou et al., 2022). The respective models of employment in themselves feed into such complexity and require deep understanding and customized management methods to handle correctly the challenges and opportunities associated with these roles. However, it is also the responsibility of healthcare settings and stakeholders to take the lead in adapting to these organizational complexities and continuously investigate new methods to improve the potentially adverse effects while creating a desirable working environment and maximum healthcare services (Devine & Ash, 2022). Collaboration and synergy between health services and education policies are essential, as they form the bedrock for sustainable pipeline development—a requisite when the supply of professionals must continuously be able to address future needs within a highly dynamic field. It is, therefore, essential that the understanding and strategic handling of these organizational complexities should be priority among policy thinkers, administrators, managers, supervisors, healthcare professionals, and educators to ensure the sustainability of healthcare delivery and to navigate the challenges of the healthcare landscape effectively. Ultimately, such committed effort and sustained commitment can turn the vision of healthcare provision into a reality.

We thank Dr. Zisis Kozlakidis for their input and editorial advice.

References

Ahmed, S., & Adams, M. (2023). Managing diversity in the workplace: Strategies for inclusive organizational culture. *Management Science Research Archives, 1*(02), 121–129.

Ajegbile, M. D., Olaboye, J. A., Maha, C. C., & Tamunobarafiri, G. (2024). *Integrating business analytics in healthcare: Enhancing patient outcomes through data-driven decision making*.

Al-Jaroodi, J., Mohamed, N., & Abukhousa, E. (2020). Health 4.0: On the way to realizing the healthcare of the future. *IEEE Access, 8*, 211189–211210.

Alowais, S. A., Alghamdi, S. S., Alsuhebany, N., Alqahtani, T., Alshaya, A. I., Almohareb, S. N., Aldairem, A., Alrashed, M., Bin Saleh, K., Badreldin, H. A., & Al Yami, M. S. (2023). Revolutionizing healthcare: The role of artificial intelligence in clinical practice. *BMC Medical Education, 23*(1), 689.

Amedari, M. I., & Ejidike, I. C. (2021). Improving access, quality and efficiency in health care delivery in Nigeria: a perspective. *PAMJ-one Health, 5*(3).

Barr, D. A. (2023). *Introduction to US health policy: The organization, financing, and delivery of health care in America*.

Bolden, R., Gosling, J., & Hawkins, B. (2023). *Exploring leadership: Individual, organizational, and societal perspectives*.

Cleverley, W. O., Cleverley, J. O., & Parks, A. V. (2023). *Essentials of health care finance*.

Constantinou, C. S., Andreou, P., Nikitara, M., & Papageorgiou, A. (2022). Cultural competence in healthcare and healthcare education. *Societies, 12*(6), 178.

Cottingham, A. H., Litzelman, D. K., Frankel, R. M., Williamson, P. R., Suchman, A. L., & Inui, T. S. (2022). The dissemination of relationship-centered care approaches to enhance the informal curriculum of academic health science centers. In *Educators' stories of creating enduring change-enhancing the professional culture of academic health science centers* (pp. 119–140). CRC Press.

Dahiyat, S. E., Khasawneh, S. M., Bontis, N., & Al-Dahiyat, M. (2023). Intellectual capital stocks and flows: Examining the mediating roles of social capital and knowledge transfer. *Vine Journal of Information and Knowledge Management Systems, 53*(1), 11–42.

Davenport, T., & Kalakota, R. (2019). The potential for artificial intelligence in healthcare. *Future Healthcare Journal, 6*(2), 94–98.

De Bem Machado, A., Secinaro, S., Calandra, D., & Lanzalonga, F. (2022). Knowledge management and digital transformation for industry 4.0: a structured literature review. *Knowledge Management Research & Practice, 20*(2), 320–338.

De Vries, N., Boone, A., Godderis, L., Bouman, J., Szemik, S., Matranga, D., & De Winter, P. (2023). The race to retain healthcare workers: a systematic review on factors that impact retention of nurses and physicians in hospitals. *INQUIRY: The Journal of Health Care Organization, Provision, and Financing, 60*, 00469580231159318.

Devine, P. G., & Ash, T. L. (2022). Diversity training goals, limitations, and promise: A review of the multidisciplinary literature. *Annual Review of Psychology*.

Dion, H., & Evans, M. (2024). Strategic frameworks for sustainability and corporate governance in healthcare facilities; approaches to energy-efficient hospital management. *Benchmarking: An International Journal.*

Dunn, J., Runge, R., & Snyder, M. (2018). Wearable sensors enable personalized predictions of clinical laboratory measurements. *Nature Medicine, 24*(6), 792–798.

Fatumo, S., Chikowore, T., Choudhury, A., Ayub, M., Martin, A. R., & Kuchenbaecker, K. (2022). A roadmap to increase diversity in genomic studies. *Nature Medicine, 28*(2), 243–250.

Ferlie, E. & Ongaro, E. (2022). *Strategic management in public services organizations: Concepts, schools, and contemporary issues*.

Filip, R., Gheorghita Puscaselu, R., Anchidin-Norocel, L., Dimian, M., & Savage, W. K. (2022). Global challenges to public health care systems during the COVID-19 pandemic: A review of pandemic measures and problems. *Journal of Personalized Medicine, 12*(8), 1295.

Gee, I. H., Nahm, P. I., Yu, T., & Cannella, A. A., Jr. (2023). Not-for-profit organizations: A multidisciplinary review and assessment from a strategic management perspective. *Journal of Management, 49*(1), 237–279.

Guillari, A., Sansone, V., Giordano, V., Catone, M., & Rea, T. (2024). Assessing digital health knowledge, attitudes and practices among nurses in Naples: A survey study protocol. *BMJ Open*.

Haleem, A., Javaid, M., Singh, R. P., & Suman, R. (2022). Medical 4.0 technologies for healthcare: Features, capabilities, and applications. *Internet of Things and Cyber-Physical Systems, 2*, 12–30.

Hermsen, M., Simons, R., van Veen, H., Prudon, A., Rooijackers, L., Otten, R., & Koordeman, R. (2024). Building high-quality interpersonal staff-client relationships with people with severe to profound intellectual disabilities and challenging behavior: Insights of professionals and relatives. *Journal of Intellectual Disabilities, 28*(1), 17–34.

Huynh, T. P. H., (2020). *The positioning of nurses in health care in Vietnam: Interactions, organisations and space*.

Junaid, S.B., Imam, A.A., Balogun, A.O., De Silva, L.C., Surakat, Y.A., Kumar, G., Abdulkarim, M., Shuaibu, A.N., Garba, A., Sahalu, Y. and Mohammed, A., (2022). Recent advancements in emerging technologies for healthcare management systems: A survey. In Healthcare (Vol. 10, 10, p. 1940). MDPI.

Khan, S., & Khan, B. (2023). The rise of telemedicine: Transforming healthcare delivery. *Open Horizon Scientific Review.*

Kruse, C. S., Smith, B., Vanderlinden, H., & Nealand, A. (2017). Cybersecurity in healthcare: A systematic review. *Healthcare (Basel), 5*(4), 88.

Li, K. C. & Wong, B. T. M., (2023). *Features and trends of personalised learning: A review of journal publications from 2001 to 2018*. Personalized learning.

Meskó, B., & Topol, E. J. (2023). The imperative for regulatory oversight of large language models (or generative AI) in healthcare. *NPJ Digital Medicine, 6*, 120.

Munoz-Gama, J., Martin, N., Fernandez-Llatas, C., Johnson, O. A., Sepúlveda, M., Helm, E., Galvez-Yanjari, V., Rojas, E., Martinez-Millana, A., Aloini, D., & Amantea, I. A. (2022). Process mining for healthcare: Characteristics and challenges. *Journal Of Biomedical Informatics, 127*, 103994.

Neelima, S., Govindaraj, M., Subramani, D. K., ALkhayyat, A., & Mohan, D. C. (2024). Factors influencing data utilization and performance of health management information systems: A case study. *Indian Journal of Information Sources and Services, 14*(2), 146–152.

Nilsen, P., Seing, I., Ericsson, C., Birken, S. A., & Schildmeijer, K. (2020). Characteristics of successful changes in health care organizations: an interview study with physicians, registered nurses and assistant nurses. *BMC Health Services Research, 20*, 1–8.

Obermeyer, Z., Powers, B., Vogeli, C., & Mullainathan, S. (2019). Dissecting racial bias in an algorithm used to manage the health of populations. *Science, 366*(6464), 447–453.

Omaghomi, T. T., Akomolafe, O., Onwumere, C., Odilibe, I. P., & Elufioye, O. A. (2024). Patient Experience and Satisfaction in Healthcare: A Focus on Managerial Approaches—A Review. *International Medical Science Research Journal, 4*, 194–209. https://doi.org/10.51594/imsrj.v4i2.812

Ozgun, A. H., Tarim, M., Delen, D., & Zaim, S. (2022). Social capital and organizational performance: The mediating role of innovation activities and intellectual capital. *Healthcare Analytics.*

Rajkomar, A., Hardt, M., Howell, M. D., Corrado, G., & Chin, M. H. (2018). Ensuring fairness in machine learning to advance health equity. *Annals of Internal Medicine, 169*(12), 866–872.

Sargsyan, K. (2023). Future of healthcare. In T. Landesz, S. Varghese, & K. Sargsyan (Eds.), *Future Intelligence. Future of Business and Finance*. Springer. https://doi.org/10.1007/978-3-031-36382-5_5

Shi, L. & Singh, D. A., 2022. *Essentials of the US health care system.*

Subrahmanya, S. V. G., Shetty, D. K., Patil, V., Hameed, B. Z., Paul, R., Smriti, K., Naik, N., & Somani, B. K. (2022). The role of data science in healthcare advancements: Applications, benefits, and future prospects. *Irish Journal of Medical Science, 191*(4), 1473–1483.

Tasheva, Z., & Karpovich, V. (2024). Supercharge human potential through AI to increase productivity the workforce in the companies. *American Journal of Applied Science and Technology, 4*(02), 24–29.

Tavakoly Sany, S. B., Behzhad, F., Ferns, G., & Peyman, N. (2020). Communication skills training for physicians improves health literacy and medical outcomes among patients with hypertension: A randomized controlled trial. *BMC Health Services Research, 20*(1), 60.

Topol, E. J. (2019). *Deep medicine: How artificial intelligence can make healthcare human again.* Basic Books.

Wiedermann, C. J., Barbieri, V., Plagg, B., Marino, P., Piccoliori, G., & Engl, A. (2023). Fortifying the foundations: a comprehensive approach to enhancing mental health support in educational policies amidst crises. *Healthcare, 11*(10), 1423.

Williams, J. H., Celaya, L. Y., Close, N., Allgood, A., Silvera, G., Borkowski, N., & Lemak, C. H. (2024). A model of inclusive excellence for health administration education. *Journal of Health Administration Education, 40*(3), 445–478.

World Health Organization. (2021). *Global strategy on digital health 2020–2025*. WHO.

Wu, Q., Jin, Z., & Wang, P. (2022). The relationship between the physician-patient relationship, physician empathy, and patient trust. *Journal of General Internal Medicine.*

MIX
Papier aus verantwortungsvollen Quellen
Paper from responsible sources
FSC® C105338
FSC
www.fsc.org

If you have any concerns about our products,
you can contact us on
ProductSafety@springernature.com

In case Publisher is established outside the EU,
the EU authorized representative is:
Springer Nature Customer Service Center GmbH
Europaplatz 3, 69115 Heidelberg, Germany

Printed by Libri Plureos GmbH
in Hamburg, Germany